Intro

Chapter 1: Fundamentals of Facebook Ads

1.1 How Facebook Ads work

1.2 Setting up an advertising account

Chapter 2: Defining Objectives and Audiences

2.1 How to set your marketing objectives

2.2 Identifying and defining the target audience

2.3 Using targeting tools in Facebook Ads Step-By-Step

Chapter 3: Creating Effective Content

3.1 The importance of quality content in Facebook Ads campaigns

3.2 How to create visually and textually compelling ads

Chapter 4: Bidding and Budgeting Strategies

4.1 Types of bidding in Facebook Ads

4.2 Setting an appropriate budget for your campaigns

4.3 Optimizing cost per action (CPA) and return on investment (ROI)

Chapter 5: Campaign Management and Optimization

5.1 Monitoring campaign performance in real-time

5.2 A/B testing to improve results

5.3 Adjusting and optimizing campaigns for better outcomes

Chapter 6: Case Studies and Practical Examples

6.1 Examples of successful Facebook Ads campaigns

6.2 Analyzing case studies for applied understanding of discussed concepts

6.3 Creative ideas and innovative strategies from real-world practice

Chapter 7: Legal and Ethical Considerations

7.1 Adhering to Facebook Ads policies and regulations

7.2 Protecting user privacy and data

7.3 Ethics in advertising and avoiding manipulative or harmful practices

Conclusions

Intro

Utilizing Facebook ads as a sales tool offers numerous advantages and opportunities for businesses looking to expand their reach, drive conversions, and maximize profitability. Here are several compelling reasons why businesses should consider using Facebook ads to sell their products or services:

1. Vast Audience Reach: With over 2.8 billion monthly active users as of January 2021, Facebook provides access to a vast and diverse audience spanning various demographics, interests, and geographic locations. This extensive reach ensures that businesses can effectively target and engage with potential customers, regardless of their niche or industry.

2. Highly Targeted Advertising: Facebook's sophisticated targeting capabilities enable businesses to pinpoint their ideal audience based on factors such as demographics, interests, behaviors, and purchase intent. This precision targeting ensures that ads are delivered to users who are most likely to be interested in the products or services being promoted, thereby maximizing the chances of conversion.

3. Cost-Effective Advertising: Facebook offers flexible and budget-friendly advertising options, allowing businesses to set their own ad budgets and bid amounts based on their specific objectives and financial constraints. Additionally, Facebook's auction-based ad system ensures that advertisers only pay when their ads are clicked or interacted with, making it a cost-effective advertising solution for businesses of all sizes.

4. Advanced Ad Formats: Facebook offers a variety of ad formats and placements to suit different marketing objectives and preferences. From image and video ads to carousel ads, slideshow ads, and more, businesses have the flexibility to choose the ad format that best showcases their products or services and resonates with their target audience.

5. Trackable Performance Metrics: Facebook provides robust analytics and reporting tools that allow businesses to track the performance of their ad campaigns in real-time. Advertisers can monitor key metrics such as reach, engagement, clicks, conversions, and return on investment (ROI), enabling them to optimize their campaigns for maximum effectiveness and ROI.

6. Remarketing Opportunities: Facebook's remarketing capabilities allow businesses to re-engage with users who have previously interacted with their brand or visited their

website but did not complete a desired action, such as making a purchase. By targeting these warm leads with tailored ads and offers, businesses can increase conversion rates and drive incremental sales.

7. Integration with E-commerce Platforms: Facebook seamlessly integrates with popular e-commerce platforms such as Shopify, WooCommerce, and Magento, allowing businesses to create a streamlined shopping experience for customers directly within the Facebook platform. This integration enables businesses to drive traffic to their online stores, promote products, and facilitate seamless transactions without users ever leaving the Facebook environment.

Overall, Facebook ads offer businesses a powerful and versatile platform for driving sales, generating leads, and achieving their marketing objectives in today's digital landscape. By leveraging Facebook's extensive reach, advanced targeting options, and robust advertising features, businesses can effectively connect with their target audience, drive conversions, and achieve sustainable growth.

Chapter 1: Fundamentals of Facebook Ads

1.1. How Facebook Ads work

Facebook Ads operates through a complex auction-based system that allows you to target specific audiences with your ads. Here's a simplified explanation of how Facebook Ads work:

Ad Creation

You create ads using the Facebook Ads Manager platform. They can choose from various ad formats such as image ads, video ads, carousel ads, etc., and specify the ad's objective, targeting criteria, budget, and schedule.

- Accessing Ads Manager:

Ad creation begins by accessing Facebook's Ads Manager or Business Manager. These platforms provide the tools necessary to create, manage, and track advertisements.

- Choosing Campaign Objective:

The first step in creating a Facebook ad is selecting the campaign objective. Facebook offers a range of objectives such as:

Brand Awareness

Reach

Traffic

Engagement

App Installs

Video Views

Lead Generation

Conversions

The selected objective aligns with the advertiser's goals and determines how Facebook optimizes ad delivery.

- Select your type campanie

Facebook currently offers users two types of campaigns: Automated and Manual. Automated campaigns are designed to streamline the advertising process by allowing the platform to handle aspects such as placement, optimization, and targeting automatically. In this case, the Facebook algorithm takes over the campaign management tasks, making decisions based on data and user behavior.

On the other hand, manual campaigns give users complete control over every aspect of your advertising campaign. They allow for more detailed customization of targeting, placements, and bidding strategies, providing greater flexibility and control over how the advertising budget is spent. The choice between the two types of campaigns depends on each user's advertising objectives and your preferences regarding the desired level of control and automation in managing your advertising campaigns.

- Advantages of Automatic Campaigns:

Dynamic Optimization: Facebook's algorithm leverages vast amounts of data to continuously optimize ad delivery. It considers factors such as audience engagement, ad relevance, and conversion likelihood to ensure ads are shown to the most receptive users.

Adaptive Targeting: Automatic campaigns allow Facebook to adjust targeting parameters dynamically based on user behavior. This adaptability can lead to improved audience reach and engagement, as the algorithm identifies and targets users with similar characteristics to those who have previously interacted with the ad.

Time Savings: Automatic campaigns streamline the setup process, eliminating the need for manual selection of placements and optimization settings. you can launch campaigns quickly and efficiently, freeing up time to focus on other aspects of your marketing strategy.

Scalability: With automatic campaigns, you can easily scale your ad spend and reach across multiple platforms and audiences. Facebook's algorithm efficiently distributes the budget to maximize campaign performance, making it suitable for businesses of all sizes.

- Advantages of Manual Campaigns:

Granular Control: Manual campaigns offer you complete control over every aspect of your ad strategy, from placement selection to bidding strategy. This level of control allows for precise targeting and optimization tailored to specific campaign objectives and audience segments.

Customized Placements: you can strategically choose where your ads appear based on performance data and audience preferences. This customization enables them to allocate budget effectively and prioritize high-performing placements to maximize ROI.

Budget Flexibility: Manual campaigns provide flexibility in budget allocation, allowing you to set bid caps or adjust bid amounts based on performance metrics. This control helps optimize ad spend and prevent overspending on underperforming placements.

Performance Transparency: With manual campaigns, you have full visibility into the performance of each placement and can make data-driven decisions to optimize campaign performance. This transparency enables them to identify trends, refine targeting strategies, and allocate budget effectively to achieve your goals.

If you opt for an automatic campaign, the subsequent steps will be streamlined, eliminating the need to navigate through every stage individually. This simplification occurs because the platform's algorithm takes on tasks such as targeting, optimization, and placement selection, allowing you to focus more on overarching strategy rather than micromanagement.

Essentially, by selecting automatic campaign settings, the process becomes more efficient and less time-consuming, granting you the convenience of a more hands-off approach to managing your ads.

If you've selected a manual campaign, after clicking the "Next" button, the four stages of a manual campaign will open. At the primary level, which is the "Campaign" level, you can make the following selections:

1. Special Ad Categories:

Declare if your ads are related to credit, employment, housing, social issues, elections, or politics. Requirements may vary by country. Accurately declaring your ad categories helps you run ads compliant with Facebook's advertising standards and helps prevent potential ad rejections.

2. Campaign Details:

Buying Type: You can specify the buying type, such as sales. At the end of this guide, you will also find an example of a traffic campaign.

Use a Catalog: Utilize a catalog to reach people most likely to engage with your products. You can also select your catalog at the ad level to use as ad creative only.

3. A/B Test:

Create A/B tests to improve ad performance by testing versions with different images, text, audiences, or placements. Each version will be shown to separate groups of your audience for accuracy.

4. Advantage Campaign Budget:

Turn on/off Advantage campaign budget, which distributes your budget across currently delivering ad sets to get more results based on your performance goal choices and bid strategy. You can control spending on each ad set.

These options allow you to customize and optimize your manual campaign according to your specific advertising goals and preferences.

- Creating Ad Set:

Within the chosen campaign, you create ad sets. Ad sets define targeting, budget, schedule, and placement options for the ads.

You can target specific demographics, interests, behaviors, and even custom audiences based on data such as email lists or website visitors.

They can further refine targeting by specifying location, age, gender, language, interests, connections, and more.

- The "Performance Goal" field allows you to specify the objective or outcome you want to achieve with your ad campaign. It helps Facebook's algorithm optimize your ads to meet your specific goal. Some common performance goals include:

Maximize Conversions: Optimize your ad delivery to get the maximum number of conversions, such as purchases or sign-ups, within your budget.

Increase Traffic: Drive more visitors to your website or landing page.

Boost Engagement: Increase likes, comments, shares, or other forms of engagement on your ads or page.

Generate Leads: Collect information from potential customers, such as email addresses or contact details.

Raise Brand Awareness: Increase the visibility of your brand or product among your target audience.

Maximize Reach: Reach as many people as possible within your target audience.

Increase App Installs: Drive more installations of your mobile app.

Promote Video Views: Increase the number of views on your video ads.

Optimize for Value: Maximize the value of conversions, such as revenue or return on ad spend (ROAS).

Selecting the appropriate performance goal aligns your campaign objectives with Facebook's optimization algorithms, helping you achieve better results for your advertising efforts.

- Audience Targeting: Define your target audience by selecting demographics (age, gender, location), interests, behaviors, connections, or custom audiences. Refine targeting further by specifying detailed targeting options, including demographics, interests, behaviors, and connections.

The "Audience Type" field allows you to specify the type of audience you want to target with your ad campaign. It provides options for how you want Facebook to deliver your ads to potential customers. Here are the common audience types available:

Broad Audience: Facebook will deliver your ads to a broad audience based on demographics, interests, and behaviors. This option is suitable for reaching a wide range of people who may be interested in your products or services.

The "Broad Audience" option allows Facebook to deliver your ads to a wide and diverse group of users based on various demographic factors, interests, and behaviors. When you select this audience type, Facebook's algorithm will optimize your ad delivery to reach as many people as possible who fit within the parameters you specify.

Here are some key features of targeting a broad audience:

1. Demographics: You can specify demographic characteristics such as age, gender, location, language, education level, and relationship status to narrow down your audience.

2. Interests: You can target users based on your interests, hobbies, activities, pages they like, or topics they engage with on Facebook.

3. Behaviors: Facebook allows you to target users based on your behaviors, such as purchase behavior, device usage, travel patterns, and more.

4. Flexibility: Broad audience targeting gives you the flexibility to reach a wide range of potential customers without overly restricting your audience criteria. This can be beneficial if you're looking to increase brand awareness or reach new customers.

5. Reach: By targeting a broad audience, you can potentially reach a larger pool of users who may be interested in your products or services, increasing the visibility of your ads and expanding your brand's reach.

6. Algorithm Optimization: Facebook's algorithm will automatically optimize your ad delivery to reach users within your broad audience who are most likely to engage with your ads or take the desired action.

Targeting a broad audience can be a strategic approach for increasing brand exposure, reaching new customers, and generating interest in your products or services. However, it's essential to monitor your campaign performance closely and refine your audience targeting based on the results to ensure optimal ad performance.

Custom Audience: A "Custom Audience" allows you to target a specific group of people who have already interacted with your business in some way. This audience is created based on your existing customer data, such as email lists, website visitors, app users, or engagement with your Facebook Page or content. Here are the key features and benefits of using a Custom Audience:

1. Targeting Specific Individuals: With a Custom Audience, you can target individuals who have already shown an interest in your business or who are part of your existing customer base. This allows you to tailor your ads to a highly relevant audience who is more likely to engage with your content and take action.

2. Multiple Data Sources: You can create Custom Audiences using various data sources, including:
   - Customer Lists: Upload your customer email lists or phone numbers to Facebook, and it will match them with Facebook user profiles.
   - Website Visitors: Install the Facebook Pixel on your website to track visitors and create Custom Audiences based on your interactions.
   - App Users: Integrate the Facebook SDK into your mobile app to track user activity and create Custom Audiences of app users.
   - Engagement with Facebook: Create Custom Audiences of people who have engaged with your Facebook Page, events, or ad content.

3. Retargeting: Custom Audiences are particularly useful for retargeting campaigns, where you can re-engage users who have previously visited your website, interacted with your app, or engaged with your Facebook content. This helps you stay top-of-mind with potential

customers and encourage them to complete a desired action, such as making a purchase or signing up for a newsletter.

4. Lookalike Audiences: Once you have created a Custom Audience, you can expand your reach by creating Lookalike Audiences. Facebook will identify users who are similar to your Custom Audience in terms of demographics, interests, and behaviors, allowing you to reach new potential customers who are likely to be interested in your business.

5. Saved Audience: You can save specific audience criteria, including demographics, interests, and behaviors, to use in multiple campaigns. This option allows you to quickly target a predefined audience without recreating it each time.

6. Dynamic Audience: Facebook will automatically create and update your audience based on real-time data, such as website visitors or interactions with your app. This option is suitable for dynamic retargeting and personalized advertising.

Selecting the appropriate audience type ensures that your ads are delivered to the right people, increasing the effectiveness and relevance of your advertising campaigns.

- Placements. Choose where your ads will be displayed across Facebook, Instagram, Messenger, and the Audience Network.. Select automatic placements for Facebook to optimize ad delivery across all available placements, or choose manual placements to select specific platforms, devices, operating systems, and placements within those platforms.

Placements refer to the locations where your ads will be displayed across Facebook's network of properties, including Facebook itself, Instagram, Messenger, Audience Network, and other partner sites and apps. Choosing the right placements is essential for maximizing the visibility and effectiveness of your ads. Here's a breakdown of the different placement options:

Automatic Placements: Facebook's default option, where your ads will be automatically placed across all available platforms and placements within those platforms. This includes

News Feed, Stories, Marketplace, Video Feeds, Right Column, In-stream Videos, Instant Articles, Instagram Feed, Instagram Stories, Messenger Inbox, and Audience Network.

Manual Placements: Allows you to select specific platforms, devices, operating systems, and placements within those platforms where you want your ads to appear. This gives you more control over where your ads are shown and allows you to tailor your placements based on your campaign objectives and audience preferences.

1. Facebook Feeds: Ads appear in users' News Feeds as they scroll through Facebook on desktop or mobile devices. This placement offers high visibility and engagement as users are actively browsing your feeds.

2. Instagram Feeds and Stories: Ads appear in users' Instagram feeds or within Instagram Stories, reaching a highly engaged audience on one of the most popular social media platforms.

3. Messenger: Ads appear in users' Messenger inbox alongside your conversations, providing an opportunity to reach users in a more private and conversational environment.

4. Audience Network: Ads appear on third-party websites and apps that are part of Facebook's Audience Network. This extends the reach of your ads beyond Facebook and Instagram to reach users across a broader network of sites and apps.

5. Right Column: Ads appear in the right-hand column of Facebook's desktop interface. This placement is less prominent than News Feed ads but can still be effective for reaching desktop users.

6. Video Feeds: Ads appear in users' video feeds on Facebook and Instagram, either as in-stream video ads or as standalone video ads.

7. Instant Articles: Ads appear within Facebook's Instant Articles, which are fast-loading, mobile-optimized articles that users can view directly within the Facebook app.

By selecting the right placements for your ads, you can ensure that they reach your target audience in the most relevant and effective manner, maximizing your campaign's performance and achieving your advertising objectives.

- Budget and Schedule. Set your ad set budget and schedule. Determine how much you want to spend and for how long your ads will run. Choose between a daily budget (the average amount you're willing to spend per day) or a lifetime budget (the total amount you're willing to spend over the entire duration of the ad set). Specify the start and end dates for your ad set or choose to run it continuously.

The "Budget and Schedule" section of your ad campaign allows you to set the financial parameters and duration for your advertising efforts. Here's a breakdown of each component:

Budget: This is the total amount of money you're willing to spend on your ad campaign. You can set your budget as a daily or lifetime budget.

 - Daily Budget: Specifies the maximum amount you're willing to spend per day on your campaign. Facebook will evenly distribute your budget throughout the day.

 - Lifetime Budget: Sets the total amount you're willing to spend over the entire duration of your campaign. Facebook will pace your spending to ensure it lasts throughout the campaign's duration.

Schedule: This allows you to specify the start and end dates for your ad campaign.

 - Start Date: The date and time when your campaign will begin running ads.

 - End Date: The date and time when your campaign will stop running ads. Alternatively, you can choose to run your campaign continuously without an end date.

Budget Scheduling: This feature allows you to schedule budget increases or decreases in advance based on certain days or times when you anticipate higher or lower sales opportunities, peak traffic periods, or other promotional time periods.

 - For example, you might increase your budget during a holiday season or special promotion to capitalize on increased consumer demand.

 - This feature helps you manage your budget more effectively and allocate resources where they're needed most.

By setting your budget and schedule strategically, you can ensure that your ad campaign runs smoothly and effectively, maximizing your return on investment and achieving your advertising goals. It's important to regularly monitor your campaign performance and adjust your budget and schedule as needed to optimize results and adapt to changing market conditions.

- Optimization and Delivery. Optimize your ad delivery for specific outcomes such as link clicks, impressions, or conversions. Facebook will deliver your ads to people most likely to take the desired action. Set a bid strategy to determine how you want to pay for your ads (e.g., cost per click, cost per impression) and how Facebook should optimize your bids.

Optimization Goal: This is the primary objective you want to achieve with your ad campaign, such as maximizing conversions, increasing website traffic, or maximizing ad recall. Facebook's algorithm will optimize the delivery of your ads to achieve this goal.
For example, if your optimization goal is to maximize conversions, Facebook will prioritize delivering your ads to users who are most likely to take the desired action, such as making a purchase or signing up for a newsletter.

Bid Strategy: This setting determines how you want Facebook to bid for ad placements to achieve your optimization goal. There are several bid strategies available, including:

Lowest Cost: Facebook will automatically bid for ad placements to get you the lowest possible cost while still achieving your campaign objectives.
Target Cost: You can set a target cost per optimization event, and Facebook will aim to get you as many optimization events as possible at or below that cost.
Bid Cap: You can set a maximum bid amount to control how much you're willing to pay for ad placements.

Ad Delivery: This setting determines how Facebook delivers your ads to your target audience. There are two options:
Standard Delivery: Facebook will deliver your ads evenly throughout the day to optimize ad spend and reach.

Accelerated Delivery: Facebook will deliver your ads as quickly as possible, which may result in spending your budget more quickly but can help maximize ad exposure.

By following these steps, you can set up an ad set on Facebook tailored to your target audience, budget, and campaign objectives.

- Ad Creative Development:

Ad creative includes visuals and text that make up the ad content. you can choose from various ad formats, including:

- **Single Image or Carousel: Static images or a series of images.**

The choice between a Single Image or Carousel ad format depends on your campaign objectives and the content you want to showcase. Here's a breakdown of each option:

The choice between a Single Image or Carousel ad format depends on your campaign objectives and the content you want to showcase. Here's a breakdown of each option:

1. **Single Image Ad:**
   - **Description:** A Single Image ad consists of a single static image accompanied by ad copy (text) and a call-to-action button.
   - **Suitability:** This format is suitable for campaigns focused on promoting a single product, service, or offer. It's also effective for highlighting a specific message or story.
   - **Benefits:**
     - Simple and straightforward: Single Image ads are easy to create and consume.
     - Quick to capture attention: With a single compelling image, you can quickly grab users' attention as they scroll through your feeds.
     - Cost-effective: Since you're only using one image, production costs may be lower compared to other formats.
   - **Best Practices:**
     - Choose high-quality, visually appealing images that align with your brand and message.

- Keep the text concise and focused on the key selling points or benefits.
- Use a clear call-to-action (CTA) that encourages users to take the desired action.

2. **Carousel Ad:**
   - **Description:** A Carousel ad allows you to showcase multiple images or videos within a single ad unit, each with its own headline, description, and CTA button.
   - **Suitability:** This format is ideal for campaigns where you want to showcase multiple products, features, or benefits. It's also effective for storytelling or guiding users through a series of steps.
   - **Benefits:**
     - Increased engagement: Users can swipe through multiple images or videos, providing a more interactive and immersive experience.
     - Showcase variety: Carousel ads allow you to highlight different products, features, or aspects of your offering, catering to diverse audience interests.
     - Drive action: Each card in the carousel can have its own CTA button, enabling users to take specific actions for each item showcased.
   - **Best Practices:**
     - Use a consistent visual theme or storytelling arc across all carousel cards.
     - Highlight the most compelling aspects of your offering in the first few cards to grab users' attention.
     - Test different combinations of images, headlines, and CTAs to optimize performance.

Ultimately, the choice between a Single Image or Carousel ad depends on your campaign goals, content assets, and audience preferences. Experiment with both formats to see which resonates best with your target audience and drives the desired results for your campaign.

- **Video: Short video clips or animations.**

Using short video clips or animations in your ads can be highly effective for capturing users' attention and conveying your message in a dynamic and engaging way. Here are some key considerations and benefits of using short video clips or animations in your ads:

1. **Attention-Grabbing:** Videos have the ability to capture attention more effectively than static images or text-based content. Short video clips or animations can quickly engage users as they scroll through your feeds, increasing the likelihood of them stopping to watch your ad.
2. **Storytelling:** Videos allow you to tell a story or convey a message in a more compelling and immersive manner. With short video clips or animations, you can showcase your product or service in action, demonstrate its features or benefits, or evoke emotions to resonate with your audience.
3. **Visual Appeal:** Well-designed animations or video clips can add visual appeal to your ads, making them more memorable and impactful. You can use animations to highlight key points, create eye-catching transitions, or add a touch of creativity to your ad creative.
4. **Versatility:** Short video clips or animations can be used across various ad formats and placements, including social media feeds, stories, in-stream ads, and more. This versatility allows you to reach your audience across different platforms and tailor your ad content to fit the context of each placement.
5. **Increased Engagement:** Video content tends to drive higher levels of engagement compared to static images or text-based content. Users are more likely to watch and interact with videos, leading to increased click-through rates, conversions, and brand awareness.
6. **Mobile Optimization:** Short video clips or animations are well-suited for mobile viewing, as they can be easily consumed on smartphones and tablets. With the majority of social media users accessing platforms via mobile devices, optimizing your ads for mobile viewing is crucial for reaching and engaging your audience.

When creating short video clips or animations for your ads, keep the following best practices in mind:

- Keep it short and concise: Aim for videos that are no longer than 15-30 seconds to maintain viewers' attention.
- Focus on the key message: Clearly communicate your value proposition or call-to-action within the first few seconds of the video.
- Use high-quality visuals and audio: Ensure that your videos are visually appealing and that any accompanying audio is clear and engaging.

- Test and iterate: Experiment with different video formats, styles, and messaging to see what resonates best with your audience, and use data-driven insights to optimize your ad performance over time.

By incorporating short video clips or animations into your ads, you can create compelling and impactful content that drives engagement, builds brand awareness, and ultimately drives results for your advertising campaigns.

- **Slideshow: A looping video created from images or video clips.**

A slideshow is a dynamic ad format that consists of a looping video created from a sequence of images or short video clips. Slideshow ads offer a visually appealing way to showcase your products, services, or brand story in a compelling and engaging manner. Here are some key considerations and benefits of using slideshow ads:

1. **Visual Storytelling:** Slideshow ads allow you to tell a story or convey a message using a series of images or video clips. You can sequence your visuals to create a narrative that captures viewers' attention and communicates your brand's key messages effectively.
2. **Cost-Effective Production:** Creating a slideshow ad is often more cost-effective than producing a full-length video. You can use existing images or short video clips, eliminating the need for expensive video production equipment or professional editing services.
3. **Ease of Creation:** Many advertising platforms, including Facebook and Instagram, offer built-in tools for creating slideshow ads. These tools typically provide templates, effects, and transitions that make it easy to create polished and professional-looking slideshows without any prior video editing experience.
4. **Engagement and Interactivity:** Slideshow ads are designed to be visually engaging and attention-grabbing. By incorporating movement, transitions, and music or sound effects, you can capture viewers' attention and encourage them to engage with your ad content.
5. **Versatility:** Slideshow ads can be used across various ad placements and formats, including social media feeds, stories, in-stream ads, and more. This versatility allows you to reach your target audience wherever they are online and tailor your ad content to fit the context of each placement.

6. **Optimized for Mobile:** Slideshow ads are particularly effective for mobile viewing, as they are designed to be lightweight and load quickly on mobile devices. With the majority of internet users accessing social media on mobile devices, optimizing your ads for mobile viewing is essential for reaching and engaging your audience.

When creating slideshow ads, keep the following best practices in mind:
- Keep it concise: Aim for a duration of 15-30 seconds to maintain viewers' attention.
- Use high-quality visuals: Choose clear, compelling images or video clips that effectively convey your message and align with your brand identity.
- Add text overlays: Include text captions or overlays to provide context, highlight key messages, or encourage action.
- Test and iterate: Experiment with different visual sequences, transitions, and calls-to-action to optimize your ad performance over time.

By leveraging the power of slideshow ads, you can create engaging and impactful ad content that drives awareness, engagement, and conversions for your business or brand.

- **Collection: A visually immersive format showcasing multiple products.**

A Collection ad is a visually immersive ad format designed to showcase multiple products or features in a single, interactive experience. Here are the key features and benefits of using Collection ads:

1. **Visually Rich Experience:** Collection ads offer a visually rich and immersive experience that combines both images and videos. This allows you to create captivating and engaging content that stands out in users' social media feeds.
2. **Showcase Multiple Products:** Collection ads are ideal for showcasing multiple products or features within a single ad unit. This is particularly useful for e-commerce businesses looking to highlight a range of products from your catalog or promote a specific product line.
3. **Seamless Shopping Experience:** Collection ads include a "Canvas" or "Instant Experience" component, which provides a seamless transition from the ad to a full-screen, interactive shopping experience. Users can browse through products, view additional images or videos, and make purchases directly within the ad unit.
4. **Increased Engagement:** The visually appealing nature of Collection ads encourages users to engage with the content and explore the featured products further. This can

lead to higher click-through rates, longer dwell times, and increased conversion rates compared to traditional ad formats.

5. **Mobile Optimization:** Collection ads are optimized for mobile viewing, making them well-suited for reaching users on smartphones and tablets. With the majority of social media users accessing platforms via mobile devices, optimizing your ads for mobile viewing is crucial for maximizing reach and engagement.
6. **Customizable Layouts:** you have the flexibility to customize the layout and design of your Collection ads to suit your brand identity and messaging. This includes choosing the arrangement of images and videos, adding text overlays, and incorporating interactive elements.
7. **Integrated Call-to-Action:** Collection ads include a prominent call-to-action (CTA) button that encourages users to take action, such as "Shop Now" or "Learn More." This helps drive traffic to your website or app and encourages users to engage with your brand further.

Collection ads offer a highly effective way to showcase multiple products or features in a visually compelling and interactive format. By leveraging the power of Collection ads, you can create engaging ad experiences that drive awareness, engagement, and conversions for your products or services.

- **Instant Experience: A full-screen mobile experience.**

Instant Experience, formerly known as Canvas, is a full-screen mobile ad experience offered by Facebook that provides an immersive and interactive way for you to engage with your audience. Here's an overview of Instant Experience:

1. **Full-Screen Immersion:** Instant Experience ads take up the entire screen of the user's mobile device, providing a captivating and immersive experience. This allows you to grab users' attention and deliver your message in a visually compelling way.
2. **Interactive Content:** Instant Experience ads can contain a variety of interactive elements, including images, videos, carousels, product catalogs, forms, and more. This interactivity encourages users to engage with the ad content and explore the brand further.
3. **Customizable Design:** you have the flexibility to customize the design and layout of your Instant Experience ads to align with your brand identity and messaging. This

includes choosing the arrangement of content, adding text overlays, and incorporating interactive elements to create a unique and engaging ad experience.

4. **Fast Loading Time:** Instant Experience ads are designed to load quickly, providing a seamless user experience without long loading times or delays. This ensures that users can access the content immediately and engage with the ad without interruption.

5. **Cross-Platform Compatibility:** Instant Experience ads are compatible with both Facebook and Instagram, allowing you to reach your audience across multiple platforms with a consistent ad experience. This helps maximize reach and engagement by targeting users wherever they are online.

6. **Tracking and Analytics:** Instant Experience ads provide robust tracking and analytics capabilities, allowing you to measure the performance of your ads and gain insights into user behavior. This includes metrics such as clicks, impressions, engagement rate, and more, enabling you to optimize your campaigns for better results.

Instant Experience offers you a powerful tool for creating immersive and interactive mobile ad experiences that drive engagement, brand awareness, and conversions. By leveraging the capabilities of Instant Experience, you can deliver compelling ad content that resonates with your audience and delivers tangible results for your business.

Ad creative should be attention-grabbing, relevant to the target audience, and aligned with the campaign objective.

Creating attention-grabbing, relevant, and goal-aligned ad creative is crucial for the success of any advertising campaign. Here's why:

1. **Attention-Grabbing:** In today's digital age, users are inundated with content vying for their attention. To stand out from the crowd, your ad creative needs to be visually compelling and engaging. This can be achieved through eye-catching imagery, bold colors, dynamic animations, or clever copywriting that piques curiosity and encourages users to stop scrolling and take notice.

2. **Relevance to Target Audience:** Understanding your target audience's needs, preferences, and pain points is key to creating ad creative that resonates with them. Your ad creative should speak directly to your audience's interests, aspirations, and challenges, demonstrating how your product or service can provide value or solve a problem for them. By tailoring your messaging and imagery to your audience's

demographics, interests, and behaviors, you can increase relevance and likelihood of engagement.

3. **Alignment with Campaign Objective:** Every advertising campaign has a specific objective, whether it's driving website traffic, generating leads, increasing sales, or raising brand awareness. Your ad creative should be aligned with your campaign objective and designed to guide users towards taking the desired action. For example, if your goal is to drive sales, your ad creative should highlight product features, promotions, and incentives to encourage users to make a purchase. By ensuring that your ad creative directly supports your campaign objective, you can maximize the effectiveness and ROI of your advertising efforts.

In summary, attention-grabbing, relevant, and goal-aligned ad creative plays a critical role in capturing audience attention, driving engagement, and ultimately achieving campaign success. By investing time and resources into crafting compelling ad creative that speaks to your target audience and supports your campaign objectives, you can create impactful advertising experiences that resonate with users and drive desired outcomes for your business.

- Ad Copywriting:

Ad copy refers to the text accompanying the ad creative, including headlines, body text, and calls-to-action (CTAs). Ad copy should be concise, persuasive, and clearly communicate the value proposition or offer.

Ad copy is the written content that accompanies the ad creative and serves to convey the message, capture attention, and prompt action from the audience. It typically includes elements such as headlines, body text, and calls-to-action (CTAs). Here's a breakdown of each component:

1. **Headlines:** Headlines are short, attention-grabbing phrases or sentences that appear at the top of the ad. They should be concise, compelling, and relevant to the ad creative and campaign objective. Headlines play a crucial role in capturing the audience's attention and encouraging them to engage further with the ad.
2. **Body Text:** Body text, also known as ad copy or ad content, provides additional context, information, or persuasion to the audience. It elaborates on the headline and communicates key messages, features, benefits, or offers related to the product,

service, or promotion being advertised. Body text should be concise, clear, and focused on addressing the audience's needs or pain points.
3. **Calls-to-Action (CTAs):** CTAs are prompts or directives that encourage the audience to take a specific action, such as "Shop Now," "Learn More," "Sign Up," or "Contact Us." CTAs should be clear, actionable, and aligned with the campaign objective. They guide users towards the desired action and help drive conversions or engagement.

Effective ad copy should be tailored to the target audience, speak to their interests or motivations, and provide a clear value proposition or benefit. It should also be consistent with the overall messaging and branding of the campaign. By crafting compelling ad copy that complements the ad creative and prompts action, advertisers can maximize the effectiveness of their advertising campaigns and achieve their desired outcomes.

You can experiment with different messaging to see what resonates best with your audience.

- Performance Tracking:

You can track the performance of your ads in real-time through the Facebook Ads Manager dashboard. They can monitor metrics such as impressions, clicks, conversions, and return on ad spend (ROAS) to evaluate the effectiveness of your campaigns.

Performance tracking refers to the process of monitoring and analyzing the effectiveness and outcomes of advertising campaigns to evaluate their success and make data-driven decisions for optimization. Here's how performance tracking works:
1. **Key Performance Indicators (KPIs):** Before launching an advertising campaign, advertisers define specific KPIs that align with their campaign objectives. These KPIs can vary depending on the campaign goals but may include metrics such as click-through rate (CTR), conversion rate, return on ad spend (ROAS), cost per acquisition (CPA), and engagement rate.
2. **Data Collection:** Advertisers use tracking tools and analytics platforms provided by advertising platforms (e.g., Facebook Ads Manager, Google Analytics) to collect data on campaign performance. These tools track various metrics in real-time, providing insights into ad impressions, clicks, conversions, and other relevant data points.
3. **Analysis:** Advertisers analyze the collected data to assess the performance of their advertising campaigns against predefined KPIs. They identify trends, patterns, and

areas of opportunity or improvement based on the data insights. This analysis helps advertisers understand what's working well and what adjustments may be needed to optimize campaign performance.

4. **Optimization:** Based on the analysis of performance data, advertisers implement optimization strategies to improve campaign effectiveness and maximize results. This may involve adjusting targeting parameters, refining ad creative and messaging, optimizing bidding strategies, or reallocating budget to high-performing ad sets or placements.

5. **Iterative Process:** Performance tracking is an ongoing process that continues throughout the duration of the advertising campaign. Advertisers continuously monitor performance metrics, make adjustments as needed, and iterate on their strategies to achieve the best possible outcomes.

6. **Reporting:** Advertisers use performance tracking data to generate reports and share insights with stakeholders, such as clients, colleagues, or management teams. These reports provide a comprehensive overview of campaign performance, including key metrics, trends, and recommendations for future actions.

UTM parameters, also known as UTM tags or tracking parameters, are snippets of text added to the end of a URL to track the performance of marketing campaigns in Google Analytics or other analytics platforms. UTM parameters help identify the source, medium, campaign name, and other relevant information about the traffic generated by a specific marketing campaign. Here's how to create UTM parameters:

URL: Start with the URL of the webpage you want to track. This could be a landing page, product page, blog post, or any other page on your website.

Campaign Source (utm_source): This parameter identifies the specific source of the traffic, such as the platform or website where the link was shared. For example, if you're running a campaign on Facebook, the source would be "facebook".

Campaign Medium (utm_medium): This parameter describes the type of traffic, such as organic search, paid search, email, social media, or referral. For example, if you're sharing the link in an email newsletter, the medium would be "email".

Campaign Name (utm_campaign): This parameter specifies the name of the marketing campaign or promotion. It helps you differentiate between different campaigns when analyzing data in Google Analytics. For example, if you're promoting a summer sale, the campaign name could be "summer_sale".

Campaign Term (utm_term): This parameter is used for tracking keywords in paid search campaigns. If you're running a Google Ads campaign, you can use this parameter to track specific keywords. If not applicable, you can leave it blank.

Campaign Content (utm_content): This parameter is used to differentiate between different versions or elements of an ad, such as different ad creatives, button colors, or ad placements. If not applicable, you can leave it blank.

Performance tracking is essential for optimizing advertising campaigns, maximizing return on investment (ROI), and achieving campaign objectives. By continuously monitoring performance metrics, analyzing data insights, and making informed decisions, advertisers can drive better results and improve the overall effectiveness of their advertising efforts.

Conclusions

A Facebook Ads campaign consists of several key elements organized in a structured manner to effectively reach your target audience and achieve your marketing objectives. Here's a breakdown of the structure and elements of a typical Facebook Ads campaign:

Campaign Level:

Objective: At the campaign level, you choose your campaign objective, which defines the primary goal of your advertising campaign. Facebook offers various objectives such as brand awareness, reach, engagement, traffic, conversions, and more.

Campaign Name: Give your campaign a descriptive name that reflects its objective and helps you identify it easily within your Ads Manager dashboard.

Ad Set Level:

Target Audience: Define your target audience at the ad set level by specifying demographics, interests, behaviors, and other criteria relevant to your target market. Utilize Facebook's advanced targeting options to reach specific audience segments effectively.

Placement: Choose where you want your ads to appear across Facebook's network of platforms and services. Options include Facebook feeds, Instagram feeds and stories, Audience Network, Messenger, and more.

Budget and Schedule: Determine your ad budget and schedule for each ad set. Set either a daily budget, which specifies how much you're willing to spend per day, or a lifetime budget, which sets a total budget for the entire ad set duration. Additionally, set start and end dates to control when your ads are shown.

Bid Strategy: Select your bid strategy, which determines how you want Facebook to optimize your ad delivery within your specified budget. Options include bid cap, target cost, lowest cost, and more.

Ad Delivery Optimization: Choose how you want Facebook to optimize your ad delivery based on your campaign objective. Options include link clicks, impressions, conversions, and more.

Ad Level:

Ad Creative: Create your ad creative by selecting ad formats (single image, carousel, video, etc.) and uploading images, videos, or other creative assets. Craft compelling ad copy that resonates with your target audience and encourages them to take action.

Ad Preview: Preview how your ad will appear to users across different placements and devices before publishing.

Call to Action (CTA): Choose a clear and relevant call-to-action button that encourages users to take the desired action, such as "Shop Now," "Learn More," "Sign Up," or "Download."

Text and Headline: Write engaging ad text and headlines that capture users' attention and communicate your message effectively. Keep your copy concise, compelling, and aligned with your campaign objective.

URL: Include a destination URL that directs users to your desired landing page or website. Ensure the URL is accurate and relevant to the ad content.

Tracking and Measurement:

Conversion Tracking: Implement conversion tracking to measure the effectiveness of your ads in driving desired actions, such as website visits, form submissions, or purchases. Set up pixel tracking or custom conversion events to track specific actions on your website.

Performance Metrics: Monitor key performance metrics such as impressions, clicks, click-through rate (CTR), conversions, cost per result, and return on ad spend (ROAS). Analyze the data to assess campaign effectiveness and optimize performance over time.

By structuring your Facebook Ads campaign with these elements, you can create targeted, compelling ad campaigns that resonate with your audience, drive engagement, and achieve your marketing objectives effectively. Regularly monitor campaign performance and make data-driven optimizations to maximize the impact of your advertising efforts on Facebook.

1.2. Setting up an advertising account

Setting up an advertising account on Facebook involves several steps to create a Business Manager account, set up payment methods, and configure account settings. Here's a detailed guide on how to do it:

- **Create a Business Manager Account:**
    - Go to the Facebook Business Manager website (business.facebook.com) and click on "Create Account."
    - Enter your business name, your name, and your business email address.
    - Follow the prompts to complete the setup process and verify your email address.

- **Add Your Business Details:**
    - Once your Business Manager account is created, click on "Business Settings" in the top right corner.
    - Navigate to the "Business Info" section and enter your business details, including business name, address, and contact information.

- **Add Your Facebook Page:**
    - In the Business Settings menu, click on "Pages" in the left sidebar.
    - Click on the "Add" button and select "Add a Page."
    - Follow the prompts to connect your Facebook Page to your Business Manager account.

- **Set Up Payment Methods:**
    - In the Business Settings menu, click on "Payments" in the left sidebar.
    - Click on "Add Payment Method" and enter your billing information.
    - You can add a credit or debit card, PayPal account, or other payment methods accepted by Facebook.

- **Configure Ad Account Access:**
    - In the Business Settings menu, click on "Ad Accounts" in the left sidebar.
    - If you already have an existing ad account, you can request access to it by clicking on "Add" and selecting "Request Access to an Ad Account."
    - If you don't have an ad account, you can create a new one by clicking on "Add" and selecting "Create a New Ad Account."

- **Set Up Ad Account Settings:**

- Once your ad account is created or connected, click on it in the Ad Accounts section.
- Review and configure the ad account settings, including currency, time zone, and ad account roles.

↓ Verify Your Domain (Optional):

To verify your domain on Facebook, follow these steps:

Access Business Settings:
Log in to your Facebook Business Manager account.
Click on "Business Settings" in the top right corner of the page.

Navigate to Brand Safety:
In the left sidebar, click on "Brand Safety" under the "Accounts" section.

Select Domain Verification:
Click on "Domains" to access domain-related settings.

Add Your Domain:
If you haven't already added your domain, click on the blue "Add" button and enter your domain name. Make sure to include the full URL (e.g., "example.com").
Click on "Add Domain."

Choose Verification Method:
Once your domain is added, find it in the list and click on the "Verify" button next to it. Facebook offers several verification methods. Choose the one that works best for you:
- ✓ DNS Verification: Add a DNS TXT record to your domain's DNS settings.
- ✓ HTML File Upload: Upload an HTML verification file to your website's root directory.
- ✓ Meta-tag Verification: Add a meta-tag to the header section of your website's HTML code.
- ✓ HTML File Upload (WordPress Plugin): Use a WordPress plugin to upload the verification file automatically.

Business Manager Email: Have Facebook send an email to an email address associated with your Business Manager account.

Follow Verification Instructions:

Depending on the verification method you choose, Facebook will provide specific instructions on what to do next.

Follow the instructions carefully to complete the verification process.

Verify Domain Ownership:

Once you've completed the verification steps, return to the Domains section of Business Settings.

Find your domain in the list and look for the verification status. It should change to "Verified" once the process is complete.

Complete Additional Steps (if necessary):

In some cases, Facebook may require additional steps to verify your domain ownership or resolve any issues that arise during the verification process.

Follow any additional instructions provided by Facebook to ensure that your domain is successfully verified.

Confirm Verification:

Once your domain is verified, you'll have access to additional features and settings within Facebook's ad platform, including enhanced brand safety controls and the ability to track conversions more accurately.

By verifying your domain on Facebook, you can ensure that your ads are compliant with Facebook's policies and provide a better user experience for your audience.

- **Invite Team Members (Optional):**

To invite team members to your Facebook Business Manager account, follow these steps:

Access Business Settings:

Log in to your Facebook Business Manager account.

Click on "Business Settings" in the top right corner of the page.

Navigate to People:

In the left sidebar, click on "People" under the "Users" section.

Invite New People:

Click on the blue "Add" button located in the top right corner.

Select "Invite New People" from the dropdown menu.

Enter Email Addresses:

In the dialog box that appears, enter the email addresses of the team members you want to invite to your Business Manager account.

Separate multiple email addresses with commas if inviting more than one person.

Choose Roles:

Next to each email address, select the role you want to assign to the team member. Roles determine the level of access and permissions they will have within your Business Manager account.

Choose from roles such as Admin, Employee, Advertiser, or Analyst, depending on the responsibilities of each team member.

You can assign multiple roles to a team member if needed.

Send Invitations:

Once you've entered email addresses and selected roles, click on the blue "Submit" button to send invitations to the team members.

Each team member will receive an email invitation to join your Business Manager account.

Accept Invitations:

Team members must accept the email invitations to join your Business Manager account. They can do this by clicking on the invitation link in the email and following the prompts to accept the invitation and create or log in to their Facebook account.

Review Pending Invitations:

After sending invitations, you can review their status in the People section of Business Settings.

Pending invitations will be listed, indicating whether they have been accepted or are still pending.

Resend or Cancel Invitations (Optional):

If necessary, you can resend or cancel pending invitations by clicking on the three dots next to each invitation in the People section.

Choose the appropriate option from the dropdown menu.

Confirm Team Members:

Once team members accept invitations and join your Business Manager account, you can see them listed under the People section with their assigned roles.

You can adjust team members' roles or permissions at any time by clicking on their name and selecting "Change Role" or "Remove" as needed.

By inviting team members to your Facebook Business Manager account, you can collaborate more effectively on managing your business's Facebook Pages, ad accounts, and other assets. Each team member can have a designated role with appropriate permissions to perform their tasks efficiently.

- **Set Up Pixel Tracking (Optional):**

To set up pixel tracking on Facebook, you'll need to create and install the Facebook pixel on your website. The Facebook pixel is a piece of code provided by Facebook that allows you to track user interactions on your website, such as page views, conversions, and custom events. Here's how to set it up:

Access Events Manager:

Log in to your Facebook Business Manager account.

Click on the "Business Tools" menu and select "Events Manager" from the dropdown.

Create a Pixel:

In Events Manager, navigate to the "Pixels" tab.

If you haven't already created a pixel, click on the "Add" button to create a new pixel.

Enter a name for your pixel and click on "Create" to generate the pixel code.

Install the Pixel Code:

After creating the pixel, you'll see a code snippet called the pixel base code.

Copy the pixel base code and paste it into the header section of your website's HTML code, just before the closing </head> tag.

Alternatively, you can use a website builder or content management system (CMS) to add the pixel code to your website. Many platforms have built-in integrations for Facebook pixel tracking.

Verify Installation:

Once you've installed the pixel code on your website, return to Events Manager.

Click on the "Test Events" button to verify that the pixel is installed correctly and tracking events on your website.

You can also use the Facebook Pixel Helper browser extension to check if the pixel is firing correctly on your website.

Set Up Standard Events (Optional):

Standard events are predefined actions that users take on your website, such as page views, purchases, sign-ups, and adds to cart.

In Events Manager, navigate to the "Data Sources" tab and select your pixel.

Click on "Add Events" to set up standard events and customize their parameters, such as event names and parameters.

Test Events (Optional):

After setting up standard events, you can test them to ensure they're tracking correctly.

Visit your website and perform the actions associated with each standard event (e.g., view a product page, add an item to the cart).

Return to Events Manager and click on the "Test Events" button to see if the events are being tracked properly.

Set Up Custom Conversions (Optional):

Custom conversions allow you to track specific actions or URLs on your website as conversion events.

In Events Manager, navigate to the "Custom Conversions" tab and click on "Create Custom Conversion."

Enter the URL or parameters for the action you want to track as a conversion, and customize the conversion settings as needed.

Review Pixel Data:

Once your pixel is set up and events are tracking correctly, you can review the data in Events Manager to analyze user behavior, measure campaign performance, and optimize your advertising strategies.

By setting up pixel tracking on your website, you can gain valuable insights into user behavior and track the effectiveness of your Facebook advertising campaigns in driving conversions and achieving your business goals

- **Review and Confirm Settings:**
    - Once you've completed all the steps, review your Business Manager settings to ensure everything is configured correctly.
    - Confirm that your ad account is active and ready to use.

By following these steps, you can successfully set up an advertising account on Facebook and start running ads to reach your target audience and achieve your business objectives.

Chapter 2.

2.1. How to set your marketing objectives

Setting clear and measurable marketing objectives is crucial for defining the purpose and success criteria of your Facebook Ads campaign. Here's a step-by-step guide on how to set your marketing objectives effectively:

- Understand Your Business Goals

Understanding your business goals through the lens of psychological marketing involves delving into the deeper motivations and emotions of your target audience. Here's how to approach it:

Emotional Connection: Identify the emotional drivers behind your customers' purchasing decisions. Psychological marketing recognizes that many buying decisions are influenced by emotions such as fear, joy, trust, or desire. Understanding the emotional needs and aspirations of your target audience can help you create marketing messages that resonate on a deeper level.

Emotional connection in psychological marketing refers to the bond formed between a brand and its audience based on shared emotions, values, and experiences. Establishing an emotional connection is essential for building brand loyalty, fostering positive associations, and influencing consumer behavior. Here's how to leverage emotional connection in your marketing efforts:

1. **Identify Core Emotions:** Determine the primary emotions you want to evoke in your target audience. These emotions should align with your brand values and resonate with your target demographic. Common emotional triggers include joy, fear, love, surprise, anger, and sadness.
2. **Tell Compelling Stories:** Use storytelling to evoke emotions and create a narrative that resonates with your audience. Share authentic stories about your brand's journey, values, and impact on customers' lives. Personal anecdotes, testimonials, and case studies can all help humanize your brand and forge emotional connections.

3. **Use Visual Imagery:** Utilize visual elements such as images, videos, and graphics to evoke emotional responses from your audience. Choose visuals that evoke the desired emotions and complement your brand message. High-quality, visually appealing content can elicit powerful emotional reactions and increase engagement.
4. **Empathy and Understanding:** Demonstrate empathy and understanding towards your audience's needs, challenges, and aspirations. Show that you genuinely care about their well-being and are committed to addressing their pain points. Empathetic marketing builds trust and strengthens emotional bonds with your audience.
5. **Create Shared Experiences:** Foster a sense of community and belonging by creating opportunities for shared experiences among your audience. Encourage user-generated content, facilitate discussions, and organize events that bring people together around common interests or values. Shared experiences deepen emotional connections and reinforce brand loyalty.
6. **Focus on Authenticity:** Authenticity is key to building genuine emotional connections with your audience. Be transparent, honest, and consistent in your communications and actions. Avoid gimmicks or manipulative tactics that may undermine trust and credibility. Authentic brands resonate more deeply with consumers and foster long-lasting relationships.
7. **Show Appreciation and Gratitude:** Express gratitude and appreciation towards your audience for their support and loyalty. Acknowledge their contributions, feedback, and testimonials publicly to demonstrate that their voices are valued. Genuine expressions of gratitude foster goodwill and strengthen emotional connections with your audience.
8. **Measure Emotional Impact:** Use metrics such as sentiment analysis, brand affinity, and emotional engagement to gauge the emotional impact of your marketing efforts. Monitor social media mentions, customer reviews, and feedback to assess how your audience is responding emotionally to your brand messaging.

Behavioral Insights: Utilize psychological principles to understand consumer behavior and decision-making processes. This includes concepts such as social proof, scarcity, reciprocity, and cognitive biases. By tapping into these psychological triggers, you can influence consumer behavior and drive action.

Here's how to apply behavioral insights in your marketing efforts:

1. **Understanding Decision-Making Processes:** Study the psychological factors that influence consumer decision-making, such as cognitive biases, heuristics, and decision-making frameworks. For example, concepts like loss aversion, social proof, and anchoring effect can significantly impact consumer behavior.
2. **Social Proof:** Utilize social proof to demonstrate that others have positively engaged with your brand or products. This can include customer testimonials, reviews, ratings, and user-generated content. Highlighting social proof can increase trust and credibility, encouraging others to follow suit.
3. **Scarcity and Urgency:** Create a sense of scarcity or urgency to prompt immediate action from consumers. Limited-time offers, exclusive deals, and countdown timers can stimulate a fear of missing out (FOMO) and drive conversions by encouraging consumers to act quickly.
4. **Anchoring Effect:** Use anchoring by presenting a high-priced option first to make subsequent options seem more reasonable in comparison. This can influence consumers' perceptions of value and increase the likelihood of them choosing a higher-priced option.
5. **Defaults and Opt-In Strategies:** Leverage default options and opt-in strategies to guide consumer behavior in a desired direction. For example, setting a default option for subscriptions or pre-selecting add-on products can increase adoption rates by reducing decision complexity.
6. **Choice Architecture:** Design your marketing materials and user interfaces in a way that guides consumers towards desired actions. This can include organizing information, simplifying choices, and highlighting key features or benefits to facilitate decision-making.
7. **Nudge Theory:** Apply principles of nudge theory to subtly encourage positive behaviors without restricting freedom of choice. Nudges can take the form of prompts, reminders, or suggestions that steer consumers towards beneficial actions, such as opting into email newsletters or completing a purchase.
8. **Behavioral Segmentation:** Segment your audience based on behavioral patterns and preferences to tailor marketing messages and offers to specific segments. Understanding how different segments respond to various stimuli allows for more targeted and effective marketing campaigns.
9. **Feedback Loops:** Implement feedback loops to provide consumers with real-time feedback on their actions and encourage desired behaviors. This can include progress

bars, rewards for completing milestones, or notifications that reinforce positive actions.

10. **Continuous Testing and Optimization:** Continuously test different messaging, offers, and strategies to identify what resonates most with your audience and drives the desired outcomes. Use A/B testing, multivariate testing, and analytics to refine your approach and maximize results over time.

By applying behavioral insights in your marketing strategies, you can better understand and influence consumer behavior, increase engagement and conversions, and ultimately drive business growth.

Segmentation: Segment your target audience based on psychological characteristics, such as personality traits, values, lifestyles, or psychographic profiles. This allows you to tailor your marketing messages and offers to specific psychological profiles, increasing relevance and resonance.

Here's how to approach segmentation:

1. **Identify Segmentation Variables:** Start by identifying the criteria you'll use to segment your audience. These variables can include demographic factors (e.g., age, gender, income, education), geographic location, psychographic characteristics (e.g., lifestyle, values, attitudes), behavioral patterns (e.g., purchase history, engagement with your brand), or firmographic data (e.g., industry, company size, job title).

2. **Analyze Your Audience Data:** Gather and analyze data about your target audience to identify commonalities and patterns. This can include data from sources such as customer surveys, website analytics, social media insights, CRM systems, and third-party data providers. Look for trends and correlations that indicate meaningful segmentation opportunities.

3. **Create Segments:** Use the segmentation variables to divide your audience into distinct segments or groups. Aim to create segments that are mutually exclusive (i.e., individuals belong to only one segment) and collectively exhaustive (i.e., all individuals are accounted for across segments). Consider factors such as size, profitability, accessibility, and responsiveness when defining segments.

4. **Develop Persona Profiles:** Once you've identified segments, create detailed persona profiles for each segment to bring them to life. Persona profiles are fictional representations of typical individuals within each segment, including demographic information, interests, motivations, pain points, and behavioral tendencies. Use

qualitative research, customer interviews, and empathy mapping to develop accurate and nuanced persona profiles.

5. **Tailor Marketing Strategies:** Customize your marketing strategies, messaging, and offers to resonate with each segment's unique needs and preferences. Develop targeted campaigns, content, and promotions that address the specific challenges, aspirations, or pain points of each segment. Personalize communications and experiences to enhance relevance and engagement.

6. **Implement Targeted Campaigns:** Deploy targeted marketing campaigns aimed at each segment, utilizing channels and tactics that align with their preferences and behaviors. Consider factors such as preferred communication channels, content formats, and timing when designing campaigns. Monitor campaign performance and adjust strategies based on segment-specific insights and feedback.

7. **Evaluate and Iterate:** Continuously monitor and evaluate the effectiveness of your segmentation efforts, using metrics such as conversion rates, engagement levels, customer lifetime value, and ROI. Identify opportunities for refinement and optimization based on performance data and feedback from each segment. Iterate on your segmentation strategy to ensure ongoing relevance and effectiveness.

Segmentation allows you to better understand and connect with your audience on a deeper level, increasing the likelihood of engagement, conversion, and long-term loyalty. By tailoring your marketing efforts to address the unique needs and preferences of each segment, you can maximize the impact of your marketing investments and drive sustainable business growth.

Brand Storytelling: Craft compelling brand stories that tap into universal human experiences and emotions. Storytelling is a powerful tool for building emotional connections with your audience and conveying your brand's values, mission, and personality.

Here's how to effectively implement brand storytelling:

1. **Define Your Brand Narrative:** Start by defining the core narrative of your brand. This narrative should encapsulate the brand's history, values, mission, and unique selling proposition. Consider what sets your brand apart from competitors and why your audience should care about your story.

2. **Identify Key Themes and Messages:** Identify the key themes and messages that you want to communicate through your brand storytelling. These themes should align with

your brand's values and resonate with your target audience. Consider the emotions you want to evoke and the action you want to inspire in your audience.

3. **Understand Your Audience:** Gain a deep understanding of your target audience, including their demographics, interests, behaviors, and preferences. Use this insight to tailor your brand storytelling to resonate with their needs, aspirations, and pain points. Consider what stories will captivate and inspire your audience, and how they will relate to your brand.

4. **Craft Compelling Stories:** Develop compelling stories that bring your brand narrative to life. Use storytelling techniques such as character development, plot, conflict, and resolution to create narratives that are engaging and memorable. Incorporate elements of authenticity, vulnerability, and empathy to connect with your audience on a human level.

5. **Use Multiple Platforms and Formats:** Tell your brand story across multiple platforms and formats to reach a wider audience and maximize engagement. This may include social media, blogs, videos, podcasts, email newsletters, and in-person events. Adapt your storytelling approach to fit the unique characteristics of each platform and format.

6. **Create Consistent Brand Messaging:** Ensure consistency in your brand messaging across all channels and touchpoints. Your brand storytelling should align with your brand identity and visual elements, creating a cohesive and recognizable brand experience for your audience.

7. **Invite Audience Participation:** Encourage audience participation and interaction with your brand storytelling. Invite them to share their own stories, experiences, and perspectives related to your brand. Incorporate user-generated content and testimonials into your storytelling to foster a sense of community and belonging.

8. **Measure and Evaluate Performance:** Monitor the performance of your brand storytelling efforts using key performance indicators (KPIs) such as engagement metrics, brand sentiment, and conversion rates. Evaluate the effectiveness of your storytelling strategies and make adjustments as needed to optimize results.

By harnessing the power of storytelling, brands can create deeper connections with their audience, build trust and loyalty, and differentiate themselves in a crowded marketplace. Effective brand storytelling has the potential to inspire action, drive brand advocacy, and ultimately contribute to long-term business success.

Customer Experience: Design customer experiences that appeal to the psychological needs and preferences of your target audience. This includes factors such as user interface design, customer service interactions, and post-purchase engagement. By creating positive emotional experiences, you can foster customer loyalty and advocacy.

Customer experience (CX) refers to the overall perception and interaction that a customer has with a brand throughout the entire customer journey, from initial awareness and consideration to post-purchase support and advocacy. It encompasses every touchpoint and interaction a customer has with a brand, including online and offline channels, products or services, customer service interactions, and brand communications. Here's how to deliver an exceptional customer experience:

1. **Understand Customer Needs:** Gain a deep understanding of your customers' needs, preferences, and pain points through market research, customer feedback, and data analysis. Use this insight to tailor your products, services, and interactions to meet and exceed customer expectations.
2. **Map the Customer Journey:** Map out the customer journey to identify key touchpoints and interactions across all channels and stages of the buying process. Understand the emotions, motivations, and barriers that customers may experience at each touchpoint, and look for opportunities to enhance their experience.
3. **Personalize Interactions:** Personalize the customer experience by leveraging customer data and segmentation to deliver relevant and targeted communications, recommendations, and offers. Use personalization techniques to make customers feel valued and understood, fostering stronger relationships and loyalty.
4. **Provide Seamless Omnichannel Experiences:** Ensure consistency and continuity across all channels and touchpoints to provide a seamless omnichannel experience. Customers should be able to transition smoothly between online and offline channels without encountering friction or disruption.
5. **Focus on User Experience (UX):** Invest in user experience design to create intuitive, user-friendly interfaces and interactions across digital platforms and touchpoints. Prioritize usability, accessibility, and aesthetics to enhance the overall customer experience and drive engagement.
6. **Deliver Exceptional Customer Service:** Provide timely, helpful, and empathetic customer service across all channels, including phone, email, chat, and social media.

Empower frontline staff with the training, tools, and authority they need to resolve customer issues quickly and effectively.

7. **Solicit and Act on Feedback:** Actively solicit feedback from customers at various stages of the customer journey and use it to identify areas for improvement and innovation. Implement feedback loops and mechanisms for capturing and responding to customer input, demonstrating that their opinions are valued and acted upon.

8. **Build Emotional Connections:** Focus on building emotional connections with customers by delivering experiences that resonate on a personal and emotional level. Use storytelling, brand values, and shared experiences to create emotional bonds that foster loyalty and advocacy.

9. **Measure and Track Performance:** Use key performance indicators (KPIs) such as Net Promoter Score (NPS), customer satisfaction (CSAT), customer effort score (CES), and customer lifetime value (CLV) to measure and track the performance of your customer experience initiatives. Use these metrics to identify successes, areas for improvement, and opportunities for innovation.

10. **Iterate and Improve Continuously:** Continuously monitor and refine your customer experience strategies based on feedback, data, and market trends. Stay agile and responsive to changes in customer needs and preferences, and be willing to iterate and experiment to deliver the best possible experience.

By prioritizing customer experience and consistently delivering exceptional experiences across all touchpoints, brands can differentiate themselves, drive customer satisfaction and loyalty, and ultimately achieve long-term success in today's competitive marketplace.

Continuous Learning: Stay abreast of developments in psychology, neuroscience, and behavioral economics to refine your understanding of consumer psychology and apply new insights to your marketing strategies. Psychology is a dynamic field, and ongoing learning is essential for staying ahead of evolving consumer trends and preferences.

Continuous learning is a fundamental aspect of personal and professional growth, allowing individuals to acquire new knowledge, skills, and perspectives throughout their lives. In the context of marketing, continuous learning is essential for staying informed about industry trends, evolving consumer behaviors, and emerging technologies. Here's how continuous learning contributes to success in marketing:

1. **Staying Updated on Industry Trends:** The marketing landscape is constantly evolving, with new technologies, platforms, and strategies emerging regularly. Continuous learning enables marketers to stay informed about industry trends, best practices, and innovations, ensuring that their skills and knowledge remain relevant and up-to-date.

2. **Adapting to Changes in Consumer Behavior:** Consumer behaviors and preferences are constantly evolving in response to cultural, social, and economic factors. Continuous learning allows marketers to stay abreast of these changes, understand shifting consumer expectations, and adapt their strategies accordingly to remain effective in reaching and engaging their target audience.

3. **Mastering New Tools and Technologies:** The rapid pace of technological advancement introduces new tools, software, and platforms that can enhance marketing efforts. Continuous learning enables marketers to master these tools, leverage data analytics, automation, artificial intelligence, and other technologies to optimize their campaigns, improve targeting, and measure performance more effectively.

4. **Exploring Emerging Strategies:** Continuous learning encourages marketers to explore and experiment with new marketing strategies and tactics. By staying curious and open-minded, marketers can discover innovative approaches to reach and engage their audience, differentiate their brand, and drive business results.

5. **Building a Growth Mindset:** Embracing a growth mindset is essential for continuous learning and development. Marketers who approach challenges with a growth mindset see setbacks as opportunities for learning and improvement, remain resilient in the face of change, and actively seek out opportunities for growth and development.

6. **Networking and Collaboration:** Continuous learning provides opportunities for networking and collaboration with peers, mentors, and industry experts. Engaging with a diverse community of professionals allows marketers to exchange ideas, share best practices, and learn from each other's experiences, fostering personal and professional growth.

7. **Enhancing Creativity and Innovation:** Exposure to new ideas, perspectives, and disciplines stimulates creativity and fosters innovation in marketing. Continuous learning encourages marketers to think critically, question assumptions, and explore alternative approaches, leading to the development of novel strategies and campaigns that resonate with audiences and drive results.

8. **Measuring and Evaluating Results:** Continuous learning includes the practice of measuring and evaluating the results of marketing efforts. By analyzing data, interpreting performance metrics, and drawing insights from campaign outcomes, marketers can identify areas for improvement, iterate on their strategies, and optimize future initiatives for greater success.

In summary, continuous learning is essential for marketers to adapt to change, embrace innovation, and drive success in a dynamic and competitive environment. By committing to lifelong learning and development, marketers can stay ahead of the curve, deliver value to their organizations, and achieve their professional goals.

By incorporating psychological principles into your understanding of business goals, you can create more effective marketing strategies that resonate with your audience on a deeper level and drive meaningful engagement and loyalty.

- Use the SMART Framework:

Apply the SMART criteria to your marketing objectives to ensure they are Specific, Measurable, Achievable, Relevant, and Time-bound. This framework helps you set clear and realistic goals that can be effectively tracked and evaluated.

1. **pecific (S):** Start by defining a specific objective or goal that clearly identifies what you want to achieve. Avoid vague or ambiguous language and focus on being precise and concise in your description. Ask yourself the following questions to ensure specificity:
    - What exactly do I want to accomplish?
    - Why is this goal important?
    - Who is involved?
    - Where will it take place?
    - What are the constraints or limitations?
2. **Measurable (M):** Establish criteria for measuring progress and success towards your objective. Determine how you will track and quantify your accomplishments. Consider the following questions to make your objective measurable:
    - How will I know when the goal is achieved?
    - What metrics or indicators will I use to measure progress?

- How much or how many?
- What is the target or desired outcome?

3. **Achievable (A):** Ensure that your objective is realistic and attainable given your resources, skills, and circumstances. Assess whether you have the necessary knowledge, abilities, and support to accomplish the goal. Consider the following questions to determine achievability:
   - Is the goal within reach, given my current capabilities?
   - Do I have access to the necessary resources and support?
   - Are there any constraints or obstacles that need to be addressed?

4. **Relevant (R):** Make sure that your objective is aligned with your broader goals, values, and priorities. Assess whether the goal is meaningful and relevant to your personal or organizational objectives. Consider the following questions to evaluate relevance:
   - Does this goal align with my long-term objectives?
   - Is it a priority for me or my organization?
   - Will achieving this goal contribute to my overall success or the success of the organization?

5. **Time-bound (T):** Establish a specific timeframe or deadline for achieving your objective. Set clear milestones or checkpoints to track your progress and keep yourself accountable. Consider the following questions to add a time-bound element to your objective:
   - When do I want to achieve this goal?
   - What is the deadline or timeframe?
   - Are there any interim milestones or deadlines?
   - What actions or steps need to be completed by when?

By following these steps and ensuring that your objectives are SMART—specific, measurable, achievable, relevant, and time-bound—you can increase your likelihood of success, maintain focus and motivation, and effectively track your progress towards achieving your goals.

- Choose Appropriate Campaign Objectives

Choosing appropriate campaign objectives is crucial for the success of any marketing campaign. Here's a step-by-step guide to help you select the right objectives:

1. **Understand Your Overall Marketing Goals:** Begin by understanding your broader marketing goals and objectives. These goals could include increasing brand awareness, generating leads, driving sales, or promoting a new product or service. Your campaign objectives should align with these overarching goals.
2. **Identify Specific Outcomes:** Determine the specific outcomes you aim to achieve with your campaign. For example, if your goal is to increase brand awareness, your objectives might include reaching a certain number of impressions or increasing website traffic. If your goal is to drive sales, your objectives might focus on increasing conversion rates or revenue.
3. **Consider the Customer Journey:** Think about where your target audience is in the customer journey and what actions you want them to take as a result of your campaign. Are you targeting customers in the awareness stage who need to be introduced to your brand, or are you targeting customers in the consideration or decision stage who are ready to make a purchase?
4. **Choose Relevant Campaign Objectives:** Based on your overall goals, specific outcomes, and the customer journey, select campaign objectives that are most relevant to your needs. Facebook offers a range of campaign objectives to choose from, including:
    - Brand Awareness: Increase awareness of your brand and reach a wider audience.
    - Reach: Maximize the number of people who see your ads.
    - Traffic: Drive traffic to your website or a specific landing page.
    - Engagement: Encourage likes, comments, shares, and other interactions with your ads.
    - Lead Generation: Collect leads by encouraging people to sign up for your email list or fill out a form.
    - Conversions: Drive specific actions on your website, such as purchases, sign-ups, or app downloads.
    - Catalog Sales: Promote products from your catalog to drive sales.

5. **Prioritize Objectives Based on Importance:** Prioritize your campaign objectives based on their importance to your overall marketing goals and the specific outcomes you want to achieve. Consider which objectives are most critical for driving the desired results and focus your efforts on those.
6. **Set Clear and Measurable Goals:** Once you've chosen your campaign objectives, set clear and measurable goals for each objective. Define specific metrics and key performance indicators (KPIs) that will allow you to track your progress and evaluate the success of your campaign.
7. **Monitor and Optimize:** Continuously monitor the performance of your campaign against your objectives and make adjustments as needed. Use the insights gained from your campaign analytics to optimize your targeting, messaging, and creative elements for better results.

By following these steps and selecting campaign objectives that are aligned with your overall marketing goals, you can create more effective and successful marketing campaigns on Facebook or any other platform.

2.2 Identifying and defining the target audience

Identifying and defining your target audience is a crucial step in creating a successful Facebook Ads campaign. Here's a detailed guide on how to identify and define your target audience effectively:

- Market Research:

Conduct thorough market research to understand your industry, competitors, and target market demographics. Gather insights into consumer behavior, preferences, needs, and pain points.
Use tools like surveys, interviews, focus groups, and social listening to gather qualitative and quantitative data about your target audience.

- Define Audience Characteristics:

Segment your target audience based on demographic factors such as age, gender, location, income level, education, occupation, marital status, and household size.
Consider psychographic characteristics such as interests, hobbies, lifestyle choices, values, attitudes, personality traits, and purchasing behavior.
Identify common challenges, desires, motivations, and pain points shared by your target audience segments.

- Create Buyer Personas:

Develop detailed buyer personas that represent your ideal customers. A buyer persona is a fictional representation of your target audience based on real data and insights.
Include demographic information, psychographic traits, preferences, goals, challenges, buying behavior, and preferred communication channels in your buyer personas.
Create multiple personas to represent different segments of your target audience, each with unique characteristics and needs.

- Understand Customer Journey:

Map out the customer journey to identify touchpoints and interactions that influence purchasing decisions. Understand how your target audience moves through the awareness, consideration, and decision stages of the buying process.

Identify key moments and channels where your target audience is most receptive to marketing messages, such as social media, search engines, websites, email, or offline channels.

- Utilize Audience Insights Tools:

Leverage Facebook's Audience Insights tool to gain valuable insights into your target audience's demographics, interests, behaviors, and purchasing habits.

Analyze data on audience size, demographics, page likes, location, activity, device usage, and more to refine your targeting strategy and reach the most relevant audience segments.

Continuously test different audience segments, messaging, creative assets, and ad formats to identify which combinations resonate best with your target audience.

Monitor ad performance metrics such as reach, engagement, click-through rate (CTR), conversion rate, and return on ad spend (ROAS) to evaluate the effectiveness of your targeting and optimization efforts.

Iterate and refine your targeting strategy based on performance data and feedback to optimize campaign performance over time.

- Stay Updated and Flexible:

Stay updated on market trends, consumer preferences, and industry developments to ensure your targeting strategy remains relevant and effective.

Be flexible and adaptive in adjusting your target audience criteria based on changing market dynamics, audience behavior, and campaign objectives.

By following these steps, you can identify and define your target audience effectively, allowing you to create highly targeted and relevant Facebook Ads campaigns that resonate with your ideal customers and drive meaningful results.

2.3 Using targeting tools in Facebook Ads Step-By-Step

Facebook Ads provides a variety of powerful targeting tools that allow you to reach your desired audience with precision. Here's how you can use these targeting tools effectively:

- Core Targeting Options:

Creating core targeting on platforms like Facebook involves selecting specific demographics, interests, behaviors, and other criteria to define your target audience. Here's a step-by-step guide to creating core targeting on Facebook:

Access Facebook Ads Manager: Log in to your Facebook Ads Manager account at business.facebook.com and navigate to the Ads Manager dashboard.

Start a New Ad Campaign: Click on the green "Create" button in the top-left corner of the Ads Manager dashboard to start a new ad campaign. Choose your campaign objective and click "Continue" to proceed to the ad set level.

Define Your Ad Set: In the ad set level, you'll define the targeting parameters for your ad campaign. Scroll down to the "Audience" section and click on "Edit" to begin defining your core targeting.

Select Location: Specify the geographic location where you want your ads to be shown. You can target countries, regions, cities, or specific postal codes. Use the search bar to find and select your desired locations.

Choose Age and Gender: Define the age range and gender of your target audience. You can target specific age groups and genders based on the demographics of your ideal customers.

Add Detailed Targeting: Use Facebook's detailed targeting options to further refine your audience based on demographics, interests, behaviors, and connections. You can target people based on factors such as:

- Demographics: Education level, relationship status, job title, etc.
- Interests: Hobbies, interests, activities, pages liked, etc.

- Behaviors: Purchase behavior, device usage, travel patterns, etc.
- Connections: People who like your Page, friends of people who like your Page, etc.

Expand Audience or Narrow Audience: Optionally, you can choose to expand your audience or narrow it down further.

- Expand Audience: This option allows Facebook to also show your ads to people who are similar to your target audience.
- Narrow Audience: This option allows you to refine your audience by adding additional targeting criteria to further narrow down your audience.

Save Your Audience: Once you've defined your core targeting parameters, you can save your audience for future use by clicking on the "Save This Audience" button.

Review and Confirm: Review your ad set settings, including your core targeting parameters, budget, schedule, and optimization settings. Once you're satisfied with your settings, click on the "Continue" button to proceed to the ad creation stage.

By following these steps, you can create core targeting on Facebook to reach your ideal audience with your ads. Tailoring your targeting parameters based on demographics, interests, behaviors, and connections can help you maximize the effectiveness of your ad campaigns and achieve your marketing objectives.

- Custom Audiences:

Creating custom audiences on platforms like Facebook allows you to target specific groups of people based on their demographics, interests, behaviors, and interactions with your business. Here's a step-by-step guide to creating custom audiences on Facebook:

Access Facebook Ads Manager: Log in to your Facebook Ads Manager account at business.facebook.com and navigate to the Ads Manager dashboard.

Navigate to Audiences: In the Ads Manager dashboard, click on the "Audiences" tab in the left-hand menu. This will take you to the Audience Manager section where you can create and manage custom audiences.

Click on "Create Audience" and **Select "Custom Audience"**: In the Audience Manager section, click on the green "Create Audience" button and select "Custom Audience" from the dropdown menu.

Choose a Data Source: Facebook offers several options for creating custom audiences based on different data sources. Choose the data source that best suits your targeting needs:

- Customer File: Upload a list of customer email addresses, phone numbers, or other identifiers to create a custom audience of existing customers.
- Website Traffic: Create a custom audience based on people who have visited your website or taken specific actions, such as viewing a particular page or making a purchase.
- App Activity: Create a custom audience based on people who have interacted with your mobile app, such as installing the app or completing specific in-app actions.
- Engagement: Create a custom audience based on people who have engaged with your content on Facebook or Instagram, such as liking your Page, watching your videos, or interacting with your ads.

Set Audience Parameters: Depending on the data source you've chosen, you'll need to set specific parameters to define your custom audience. For example:

- If you're creating a customer file audience, you'll upload your customer list and match it to Facebook users based on their email addresses or phone numbers.
- If you're creating a website traffic audience, you'll define criteria such as website visitors within a specific timeframe or visitors who have performed specific actions on your site.
- If you're creating an engagement audience, you'll specify the types of engagement you want to target, such as people who have watched a certain percentage of your video or clicked on your ad.

Name Your Audience: Give your custom audience a descriptive name that reflects its criteria and purpose. This will make it easier to identify and manage your audiences in the future.

Create Your Audience: Once you've set your audience parameters and named your audience, click on the "Create Audience" button to create your custom audience. Facebook will process your audience and make it available for use in your ad campaigns.

Use Your Custom Audience in Ad Campaigns: After creating your custom audience, you can use it to target your ads to specific groups of people in your ad campaigns. When creating or editing a campaign, ad set, or ad, you'll have the option to select your custom audience under the "Audience" targeting section.

By following these steps, you can create custom audiences on Facebook to target specific groups of people based on their characteristics, behaviors, and interactions with your business. Custom audiences can help you reach the right people with your ads and maximize the effectiveness of your marketing campaigns.

- Lookalike Audiences:

Creating lookalike audiences on platforms like Facebook allows you to target new users who are similar to your existing customers or audience. Here's a step-by-step guide to creating lookalike audiences on Facebook:

Access Facebook Ads Manager: Log in to your Facebook Ads Manager account at business.facebook.com and navigate to the Ads Manager dashboard.

Navigate to Audiences: In the Ads Manager dashboard, click on the "Audiences" tab in the left-hand menu. This will take you to the Audience Manager section where you can create and manage audiences.

Click on "Create Audience" and Select **"Lookalike Audience"**: In the Audience Manager section, click on the green "Create Audience" button and select "Lookalike Audience" from the dropdown menu.

Choose a Source Audience: Select the source audience that you want Facebook to use as the basis for creating the lookalike audience. The source audience should be a custom audience that represents your existing customers, website visitors, or engaged users. You can also choose to create a lookalike audience based on your Facebook Page fans.

Select the Location and Audience Size: Specify the location for your lookalike audience. You can choose to create a lookalike audience for a specific country, region, or city. Additionally, you can adjust the audience size using a sliding scale from 1% to 10%, with 1% representing the top 1% of people in your selected location who are most similar to your source audience.

Name Your Audience: Give your lookalike audience a descriptive name that reflects its source audience and location. This will make it easier to identify and manage your audiences in the future.

Create Your Lookalike Audience: Once you've chosen your source audience, location, and audience size, click on the "Create Audience" button to create your lookalike audience. Facebook will process your audience and make it available for use in your ad campaigns.

Use Your Lookalike Audience in Ad Campaigns: After creating your lookalike audience, you can use it to target your ads to new users who are similar to your existing audience. When creating or editing a campaign, ad set, or ad, you'll have the option to select your lookalike audience under the "Audience" targeting section.

By following these steps, you can create lookalike audiences on Facebook to target new users who share characteristics and behaviors with your existing customers or audience. Lookalike audiences can help you expand your reach and find new customers who are likely to be interested in your products or services.

- Detailed Targeting:

Combine multiple targeting criteria to create highly specific audience segments. Use AND/OR logic to narrow down your audience based on specific demographics, interests, behaviors, or connections.

Refine your audience targeting by excluding certain demographics, interests, or behaviors that are not relevant to your campaign objectives.

Here's a step-by-step guide to combining targeting criteria:

Access Facebook Ads Manager: Log in to your Facebook Ads Manager account at business.facebook.com.

Start a New Ad Campaign: Click on the "Create" button to start a new ad campaign.

Choose Your Campaign Objective: Select the campaign objective that aligns with your advertising goals, such as brand awareness, traffic, conversions, etc. Click "Continue" to proceed to the ad set level.

Set Up Your Ad Set:
- Name your ad set to reflect the audience segment you're targeting.
- Scroll down to the "Audience" section.

Select Custom Audiences or Detailed Targeting:
- Choose "Custom Audiences" if you want to target users from existing customer lists, website visitors, app users, etc.
- Choose "Detailed Targeting" if you want to target users based on demographics, interests, behaviors, etc.

Combine Targeting Criteria:
- If you selected "Custom Audiences," choose the custom audience(s) you want to target.
- If you selected "Detailed Targeting," start by selecting one targeting criterion (e.g., demographics).
- Click on "Browse" to explore additional targeting options or enter specific interests, behaviors, or demographics in the search bar.
- To add multiple targeting criteria, click on "Narrow Audience" at the bottom of the detailed targeting section. This allows you to refine your audience further by adding additional criteria.

Refine Your Audience:

- Continue adding targeting criteria based on your audience segmentation strategy.
- Use the audience size gauge on the right side of the targeting section to monitor how your selections impact audience size. Aim for a balance between specificity and reach.

Review and Confirm:
- Review all the settings of your ad set, including targeting criteria, budget, schedule, and placements.
- Ensure that your audience segment is highly specific and aligned with your campaign objectives.
- Make any necessary adjustments and click "Continue" to proceed to the ad creation stage.

Create Your Ad Creative:
- Design compelling ad creatives that resonate with your highly specific audience segment.
- Write ad copy that speaks directly to the interests, needs, and pain points of your target audience.

Publish Your Ad:
- Once you've created your ad creative, review all the settings one final time.
- Click on the "Publish" button to launch your ad campaign and start reaching your highly specific audience segment.

By combining multiple targeting criteria, you can create highly specific audience segments on Facebook that are more likely to resonate with your ads and drive desired outcomes.

- Dynamic Audiences:

Set up dynamic ad campaigns that automatically adjust targeting criteria based on user behavior and preferences. Dynamic ads show personalized content to users based on your interactions with your website, app, or Facebook Page.

- Retargeting Campaigns:

Set up retargeting campaigns to re-engage users who have previously interacted with your brand but did not complete a desired action, such as making a purchase or signing up for a newsletter. Use custom audiences to target these users with relevant ads and incentives to encourage them to convert.

Before starting, ensure you have the following:

Meta Pixel or App Events: Install a pixel on your website to track standard events, such as product views, items added to the basket, or purchases. Alternatively, use app events if you have a mobile app.

Catalog: If supported, you can utilize a data feed from a partner integration (e.g., Shopify) to set up your catalog.

Retargeting an Audience

To retarget an audience for your Advantage+ catalog ad:
1. Open Meta Ads Manager and either create your Advantage+ catalog ad campaign or edit an existing one.
2. In the Audience section at the Ad Set level, choose "Retarget ads to people who interacted with your products on and off Facebook."
3. Select a Catalog interaction and adjust the number of days. You can also specify the products to include.
4. If you opt for a Custom combination, specify Included audience interactions. For example:
    - Users who added a product to cart in the last 45 days
    - But did not make a purchase in the last 45 days
5. (Optional) Under Custom audiences, you can add custom audiences and lookalike audiences.
6. Choose:
    - "Also" to add all people in any added audience to your total audience.
    - "Only" to restrict your audience to people who are both in your added audience and who have completed your selected Catalog interaction.

7. (Optional) Check "Expand audiences" to broaden your reach beyond selected custom audiences, lookalike audiences, and Catalog interactions if it's likely to improve performance.
8. (Optional) Select "Show more options" to exclude demographics such as Locations, Age, or Gender.
9. Your ad will retarget your audience and potentially reach people beyond it.

Note: When your audience is expanded through Advantage products, the estimated audience size may not reflect the total number of Accounts Center accounts that meet the targeting criteria.

- Audience Insights:

Use Facebook's Audience Insights tool to gain valuable insights into your target audience's demographics, interests, behaviors, and purchasing habits. Analyze data on audience size, demographics, page likes, location, activity, device usage, and more to refine your targeting strategy and reach the most relevant audience segments.

By leveraging these targeting tools effectively, you can create highly targeted Facebook Ads campaigns that reach the right audience with the right message at the right time, leading to improved campaign performance, higher engagement, and increased return on investment (ROI).

Chapter 3: Creating Effective Content

3.1. The importance of quality content in Facebook Ads campaigns

The importance of quality content in Facebook Ads campaigns cannot be overstated. Here are several key reasons why high-quality content is essential for the success of your Facebook Ads campaigns:

 Capturing Attention

Quality content grabs the attention of users as they scroll through your Facebook feeds. Compelling visuals, engaging copy, and captivating videos are more likely to stand out and capture users' interest, increasing the chances of them stopping to engage with your ad.

Capturing attention is crucial for the success of Facebook Ads campaigns. Here's why:
1. **Scrolling Behavior:** Users scroll rapidly through their Facebook feeds, making it challenging for ads to grab their attention. Captivating content is essential to stand out amidst the sea of other posts.
2. **First Impression:** In the competitive digital landscape, you have only a few seconds to make a lasting impression. Attention-grabbing visuals, such as striking images or engaging videos, can compel users to pause and explore your ad further.
3. **Content Relevance:** Tailoring your content to resonate with your target audience increases the likelihood of capturing their attention. Understanding your audience's interests, preferences, and pain points allows you to create content that speaks directly to them.
4. **Creative Elements:** Incorporating creative elements like bold colors, compelling headlines, and dynamic animations can help your ad stand out and capture attention quickly. Experimenting with different creative formats allows you to discover what resonates most with your audience.
5. **Value Proposition:** Clearly communicating the value proposition of your product or service within the first few seconds of your ad is crucial. Highlighting the benefits and unique selling points upfront can capture users' attention and encourage them to engage further.

6. **Mobile Optimization:** Given that a significant portion of Facebook users access the platform via mobile devices, optimizing your ad content for mobile viewing is essential. Ensuring that your visuals and copy are concise, visually appealing, and load quickly on mobile devices improves the chances of capturing users' attention.

In summary, capturing attention is the first step towards achieving success in Facebook Ads campaigns. By creating visually compelling content, tailoring it to your audience's interests, and communicating your value proposition effectively, you can increase the likelihood of capturing users' attention and driving meaningful engagement with your ads.

- *Building Trust and Credibility*

High-quality content helps to build trust and credibility with your audience. When users encounter ads that provide valuable information, solve your problems, or entertain them, they are more likely to perceive your brand positively and view you as a trustworthy authority in your industry.

Building trust and credibility is essential for the success of Facebook Ads campaigns. Here's why it matters:

1. **Brand Perception:** Trustworthy and credible ads contribute to a positive perception of your brand. When users encounter ads that are transparent, authentic, and reliable, they are more likely to view your brand favorably and consider engaging with your products or services.
2. **Audience Engagement:** Trustworthy ads are more likely to resonate with your target audience and encourage them to engage. When users trust the information presented in your ads, they are more inclined to like, comment, share, or click through to learn more.
3. **Long-Term Relationships:** Building trust and credibility through your ads lays the foundation for long-term relationships with your audience. When users trust your brand, they are more likely to become repeat customers and advocates who recommend your products or services to others.
4. **Reduced Skepticism:** In an era where skepticism towards advertising is prevalent, trustworthy ads stand out. By providing accurate information, addressing potential

concerns, and delivering on promises, you can alleviate skepticism and foster trust among your audience.

5. **Brand Loyalty:** Trustworthy brands earn the loyalty of their customers. When users have confidence in your brand's integrity and reliability, they are more likely to choose your products or services over competitors' offerings and remain loyal to your brand over time.

6. **Positive Reviews and Referrals:** Trustworthy brands are more likely to receive positive reviews and referrals from satisfied customers. Word-of-mouth recommendations and online reviews play a significant role in shaping consumers' purchasing decisions, making trustworthiness a valuable asset for generating organic growth.

In summary, building trust and credibility in Facebook Ads campaigns is essential for fostering positive brand perception, encouraging audience engagement, nurturing long-term relationships, reducing skepticism, fostering brand loyalty, and generating positive reviews and referrals. By prioritizing transparency, authenticity, and reliability in your ad content, you can establish your brand as trustworthy and credible in the eyes of your audience.

Enhancing User Experience

Quality content contributes to a positive user experience on Facebook. Ads that are well-designed, informative, and relevant to users' interests are less likely to be perceived as intrusive or disruptive. Instead, they seamlessly integrate into users' feeds and provide value, enhancing overall user satisfaction.

Enhancing user experience is crucial for the success of Facebook Ads campaigns. Here's why it matters:

1. **Positive Interaction:** Ads that offer a seamless and enjoyable experience for users are more likely to be well-received. When users have a positive interaction with your ad, they are more inclined to engage with your content and take the desired action.

2. **Relevance:** Tailoring your ads to be relevant to your target audience enhances the user experience by providing content that meets their needs and interests. By understanding your audience's preferences and delivering personalized messaging, you can increase engagement and drive conversions.

3. **Fast Loading Times:** Users expect ads to load quickly and smoothly, especially on mobile devices. Ensuring that your ad content loads promptly and is optimized for different devices and connection speeds improves the overall user experience and reduces the likelihood of users abandoning your ad.
4. **Clear Call-to-Action (CTA):** A clear and compelling call-to-action prompts users to take the desired action, whether it's making a purchase, signing up for a newsletter, or visiting your website. By providing a straightforward path for users to follow, you streamline the user experience and increase the likelihood of conversions.
5. **Mobile Optimization:** Given that a significant portion of Facebook users access the platform via mobile devices, optimizing your ads for mobile viewing is essential. Mobile-optimized ads with responsive design and easy navigation enhance the user experience and ensure that users can engage with your content seamlessly on any device.
6. **Value-Driven Content:** Providing valuable and informative content in your ads enhances the user experience by delivering relevant and engaging information. By focusing on solving users' problems or addressing their needs, you demonstrate the value of your products or services and establish credibility with your audience.

In summary, enhancing user experience in Facebook Ads campaigns is essential for driving engagement, increasing conversions, and building positive brand perception. By prioritizing relevance, fast loading times, clear CTAs, mobile optimization, and value-driven content, you can create ads that resonate with your audience and deliver a seamless and enjoyable experience.

- *Driving Engagement*

Quality content encourages user engagement with your ads. Whether it's liking, commenting, sharing, or clicking through to your website, compelling content sparks interaction and encourages users to take action. Higher engagement rates indicate that your ads are resonating with your target audience and generating interest in your brand.

Enhancing user experience is crucial for the success of Facebook Ads campaigns. Here's why it matters:

1. **Positive Interaction:** Ads that offer a seamless and enjoyable experience for users are more likely to be well-received. When users have a positive interaction with your ad, they are more inclined to engage with your content and take the desired action.
2. **Relevance:** Tailoring your ads to be relevant to your target audience enhances the user experience by providing content that meets their needs and interests. By understanding your audience's preferences and delivering personalized messaging, you can increase engagement and drive conversions.
3. **Fast Loading Times:** Users expect ads to load quickly and smoothly, especially on mobile devices. Ensuring that your ad content loads promptly and is optimized for different devices and connection speeds improves the overall user experience and reduces the likelihood of users abandoning your ad.
4. **Clear Call-to-Action (CTA):** A clear and compelling call-to-action prompts users to take the desired action, whether it's making a purchase, signing up for a newsletter, or visiting your website. By providing a straightforward path for users to follow, you streamline the user experience and increase the likelihood of conversions.
5. **Mobile Optimization:** Given that a significant portion of Facebook users access the platform via mobile devices, optimizing your ads for mobile viewing is essential. Mobile-optimized ads with responsive design and easy navigation enhance the user experience and ensure that users can engage with your content seamlessly on any device.
6. **Value-Driven Content:** Providing valuable and informative content in your ads enhances the user experience by delivering relevant and engaging information. By focusing on solving users' problems or addressing their needs, you demonstrate the value of your products or services and establish credibility with your audience.

In summary, enhancing user experience in Facebook Ads campaigns is essential for driving engagement, increasing conversions, and building positive brand perception. By prioritizing relevance, fast loading times, clear CTAs, mobile optimization, and value-driven content, you can create ads that resonate with your audience and deliver a seamless and enjoyable experience.

Increasing Conversion Rates

Well-crafted content has the power to drive conversions and sales. By providing users with relevant information, addressing your pain points, and highlighting the benefits of your products or services, quality content motivates users to take the desired action, such as making a purchase, signing up for a newsletter, or requesting more information.

Increasing conversion rates is a primary objective for most Facebook Ads campaigns. Here are several strategies to achieve this goal:

1. **Targeted Audience:** Ensure that your ads are reaching the right audience segment. Utilize Facebook's targeting options to narrow down your audience based on demographics, interests, behaviors, and other relevant criteria. By targeting users who are more likely to be interested in your products or services, you increase the chances of converting them.
2. **Compelling Offer:** Create an irresistible offer that incentivizes users to take action. Whether it's a discount, promotion, free trial, or exclusive deal, make sure your offer provides clear value to the audience. Highlight the benefits of your offer in your ad copy to entice users to click through and convert.
3. **Clear Call-to-Action (CTA):** Use a clear and prominent call-to-action (CTA) in your ads to guide users towards the desired action. Whether it's "Shop Now," "Sign Up," "Learn More," or "Download Now," ensure that your CTA is compelling and aligned with your campaign objective.
4. **Compelling Ad Creative:** Create visually appealing ad creative that grabs users' attention and communicates your message effectively. Use high-quality images or videos, attention-grabbing headlines, and concise yet compelling ad copy to persuade users to take action.
5. **Landing Page Optimization:** Ensure that your landing page is optimized for conversions. The landing page should be relevant to the ad content, load quickly, and provide a seamless user experience. Remove any distractions and make it easy for users to complete the desired action, whether it's making a purchase, filling out a form, or signing up for a newsletter.
6. **A/B Testing:** Experiment with different ad creatives, copy variations, offers, and targeting options to identify what resonates best with your audience. Conduct A/B tests to compare the performance of different elements and optimize your campaigns based on the results.

7. **Remarketing:** Implement remarketing campaigns to re-engage users who have previously interacted with your brand but did not convert. Show them tailored ads with personalized messaging to encourage them to revisit your website and complete the desired action.
8. **Optimize Ad Placement:** Test different ad placements to determine which ones drive the highest conversion rates. Whether it's in the Facebook News Feed, Instagram Stories, or the Audience Network, identify the placements that deliver the best results for your campaign objectives.

By implementing these strategies, you can increase conversion rates and maximize the effectiveness of your Facebook Ads campaigns. Continuously monitor and optimize your campaigns based on performance data to drive even better results over time.

Optimizing Ad Performance: Quality content contributes to better ad performance metrics. Ads with high-quality content typically have higher click-through rates (CTR), lower bounce rates, and improved conversion rates, leading to a higher return on investment (ROI) for your Facebook Ads campaigns.

- *Differentiating Your Brand*

In a crowded digital landscape, quality content helps your brand stand out from the competition. By delivering unique, informative, and memorable content, you differentiate your brand and create a distinct identity that resonates with your target audience.

Differentiating your brand is crucial in a competitive marketplace to stand out and attract customers. Here are some strategies to effectively differentiate your brand:

1. **Identify Your Unique Value Proposition (UVP):** Define what sets your brand apart from competitors and why customers should choose you over alternatives. Your UVP should highlight the unique benefits, features, or qualities that make your brand special and valuable to your target audience.
2. **Understand Your Target Audience:** Conduct market research to gain insights into your target audience's needs, preferences, and pain points. Tailor your products, services, and messaging to address specific customer needs and offer solutions that resonate with your audience.

3. **Create Compelling Brand Messaging:** Develop a strong brand narrative and messaging that communicates your UVP clearly and effectively. Craft a compelling brand story that resonates with your target audience's emotions, values, and aspirations, and use consistent messaging across all touchpoints to reinforce your brand identity.
4. **Focus on Brand Experience:** Prioritize delivering exceptional brand experiences at every customer touchpoint, from the first interaction to post-purchase support. Provide a seamless and memorable experience that exceeds customer expectations and leaves a lasting impression.
5. **Offer Unique Products or Services:** Develop innovative products or services that address unmet needs in the market or offer a unique solution to common problems. Differentiate your offerings by introducing distinctive features, designs, or functionalities that set them apart from competitors.
6. **Emphasize Brand Personality and Values:** Infuse your brand with a distinct personality and set of values that resonate with your target audience. Communicate your brand's personality through visual elements, tone of voice, and brand messaging, and align your values with those of your customers to build trust and authenticity.
7. **Provide Outstanding Customer Service:** Offer exceptional customer service that goes above and beyond to delight customers and exceed their expectations. Invest in training your customer service team to provide personalized, responsive, and empathetic support that fosters positive relationships with customers.
8. **Build Brand Recognition:** Invest in building brand awareness and recognition through strategic marketing initiatives, including advertising, social media, content marketing, and public relations. Consistently reinforce your brand identity and messaging to increase visibility and stay top-of-mind with your target audience.
9. **Monitor and Adapt to Market Trends:** Stay informed about market trends, industry developments, and changes in customer preferences, and be agile in adapting your brand strategy accordingly. Continuously evaluate your competitive landscape and adjust your positioning to maintain relevance and differentiation in the market.

By implementing these strategies, you can effectively differentiate your brand, attract customers, and build long-term relationships that drive loyalty and growth.

In conclusion, quality content is fundamental to the success of Facebook Ads campaigns. It not only captures attention, builds trust, and drives engagement but also enhances the user experience, increases conversion rates, and fosters brand loyalty. By prioritizing quality content creation in your Facebook Ads campaigns, you can maximize the impact of your advertising efforts and achieve your marketing objectives more effectively.

3.2 How to create visually and textually compelling ads

Creating visually and textually compelling ads is essential for grabbing the attention of your audience and driving engagement on Facebook. Here's a step-by-step guide on how to create ads that are both visually and textually appealing:

Understand Your Audience:

Start by understanding your target audience's demographics, interests, preferences, and pain points. Tailor your ad content to resonate with your needs and motivations.
Define Your Unique Selling Proposition (USP):

Identify what sets your products or services apart from the competition. Highlight your unique value proposition in your ad copy and visuals to capture the attention of your audience.

Craft Compelling Ad Copy:

Write concise and compelling ad copy that communicates your message clearly and persuasively. Use attention-grabbing headlines, benefit-driven language, and a strong call-to-action (CTA) to encourage users to take action.
Keep your copy focused on the benefits and solutions your products or services offer to your target audience. Use language that resonates with your needs and emotions.

Use High-Quality Visuals:

Choose visually appealing images or videos that showcase your products or services in the best light. Use high-resolution images and videos that are clear, crisp, and professionally shot. Select visuals that evoke emotion, tell a story, or capture the attention of your audience. Consider using lifestyle imagery that shows your products in real-life situations or user-generated content (UGC) that features satisfied customers.
Experiment with different formats such as single images, carousels, slideshows, or videos to see what resonates best with your audience.

Focus on Branding and Consistency:

Ensure that your ads reflect your brand's visual identity and messaging guidelines. Use consistent colors, fonts, and imagery across all your ad creatives to reinforce brand recognition and establish a cohesive brand image.

Incorporate your logo and brand elements strategically within your ad creatives to reinforce brand association and credibility.

Optimize for Mobile:

Design your ads with mobile users in mind, as the majority of Facebook users access the platform on mobile devices. Ensure that your visuals and text are legible and impactful on smaller screens.

Test your ad creatives on various mobile devices to ensure they render correctly and deliver a seamless user experience.

A/B Testing:

Experiment with different ad creatives, headlines, copy variations, and visual elements to identify what resonates best with your audience. Conduct A/B tests to compare performance metrics and optimize your ads for better results.

Test different combinations of visuals and copy to determine which combinations drive higher engagement, click-through rates (CTR), and conversions.

Monitor and Iterate:

Regularly monitor the performance of your ads using Facebook Ads Manager. Track key metrics such as impressions, clicks, CTR, conversions, and return on ad spend (ROAS).

Use performance data to identify trends, insights, and areas for improvement. Continuously iterate and refine your ad creatives based on performance feedback to maximize effectiveness and achieve your campaign objectives.

By following these steps and implementing best practices, you can create visually and textually compelling ads that resonate with your audience, drive engagement, and achieve your marketing goals on Facebook.

Chapter 4: Bidding and Budgeting Strategies

4.1 Types of bidding in Facebook Ads

In Facebook Ads, you have several options for bidding strategies to optimize your ad campaigns and achieve your marketing objectives. Here are the main types of bidding strategies available on Facebook Ads:

- *Lowest Cost (Automatic Bidding)*

With the Lowest Cost bidding strategy, Facebook automatically bids on behalf of the advertiser to get the most results (such as link clicks or impressions) at the lowest possible cost.
This bidding strategy is suitable for you who want to maximize your campaign's reach and are less concerned about controlling costs.

"Lowest Cost (Automatic Bidding)" refers to a bidding strategy available in Facebook Ads Manager that aims to get you the most results at the lowest possible cost. When using this bidding strategy, Facebook's algorithm automatically adjusts your bid to help you achieve the lowest cost per result based on your campaign objective and budget.

Here's how the "Lowest Cost" bidding strategy works:
1. **Automatic Optimization:** Facebook's algorithm automatically optimizes your bids in real-time to deliver your ads to the people most likely to take the desired action at the lowest cost per result.
2. **Maximizing Results:** The goal of this bidding strategy is to maximize the number of results (e.g., link clicks, conversions, app installs) you get within your specified budget. Facebook aims to deliver your ads to the most relevant audience segments where it's most likely to generate results efficiently.
3. **Budget Control:** You set a daily or lifetime budget for your campaign, and Facebook's algorithm manages your bids to ensure you stay within that budget while maximizing results.

4. **Performance Monitoring:** It's important to monitor the performance of your ads regularly when using the Lowest Cost bidding strategy. Keep an eye on key metrics such as cost per result, conversion rate, and return on ad spend (ROAS) to assess the effectiveness of your campaign and make any necessary adjustments.
5. **Campaign Objective Alignment:** This bidding strategy works best when aligned with specific campaign objectives such as traffic, conversions, app installs, or lead generation. Facebook's algorithm will optimize bids based on the specific action you want people to take.
6. **Learning Phase:** When you first start using the Lowest Cost bidding strategy or make significant changes to your campaign, Facebook's algorithm enters a learning phase where it gathers data and adjusts bidding strategies to optimize performance. During this phase, it's normal to see fluctuations in performance until the algorithm learns and stabilizes.

Overall, the Lowest Cost (Automatic Bidding) strategy can be an effective way to optimize your Facebook Ads campaigns for maximum results while maintaining control over your budget. However, it's important to closely monitor performance and make adjustments as needed to ensure your campaign objectives are being met efficiently.

Cost Cap

Cost Cap bidding allows you to set a maximum limit on the average cost per optimization event, such as cost per click (CPC) or cost per conversion.

Facebook will try to keep the cost per optimization event below the specified cost cap while maximizing the number of results achieved.

This bidding strategy is suitable for you who want to control costs while still optimizing for specific actions or conversions.

Here's how the Cost Cap bidding strategy works:
1. **Setting a Maximum Cost:** With Cost Cap bidding, advertisers specify the maximum amount they are willing to pay for each optimization event, such as link clicks, conversions, or app installs. This maximum cost is defined by the advertiser and represents the upper limit of what they are willing to spend per result.
2. **Automatic Bid Optimization:** Facebook's algorithm automatically adjusts bids in real-time to help advertisers achieve the lowest possible cost per optimization event

while staying within the specified cost cap. The algorithm optimizes bids based on factors such as audience engagement, ad relevance, and competition in the auction.

3. **Budget Control:** Advertisers also set a daily or lifetime budget for their campaign, which helps control overall advertising costs. The cost cap ensures that advertisers do not exceed their maximum cost per optimization event, helping them maintain control over their advertising expenses.

4. **Campaign Objective Alignment:** Cost Cap bidding works best when aligned with specific campaign objectives, such as conversions, app installs, or lead generation. Advertisers specify the optimization event they want to optimize for, and Facebook's algorithm adjusts bids accordingly to achieve the desired results at or below the specified cost cap.

5. **Performance Monitoring:** It's important for advertisers to monitor the performance of their ads regularly when using the Cost Cap bidding strategy. They should track key metrics such as cost per result, conversion rate, and return on ad spend (ROAS) to assess the effectiveness of their campaign and make any necessary adjustments.

6. **Learning Phase:** Similar to other bidding strategies, Cost Cap bidding may enter a learning phase when first implemented or when significant changes are made to the campaign. During this phase, Facebook's algorithm gathers data and adjusts bidding strategies to optimize performance. Advertisers may see fluctuations in performance until the algorithm stabilizes.

Overall, the Cost Cap bidding strategy provides advertisers with a way to control their advertising costs while still achieving their campaign objectives. By setting a maximum cost per optimization event, advertisers can ensure that they are getting the most value from their ad spend while staying within their budget constraints.

- *Bid Cap*

Bid Cap bidding allows you to set a maximum bid amount for your ad auctions. Facebook will not bid higher than the specified bid cap in auctions.

This bidding strategy gives you more control over your bid amounts and allows them to prioritize certain auctions or placements where they want your ads to appear.
you should set bid caps based on your desired cost per result and the value they place on different actions or conversions.

Here's how Bid Cap works:
1. **Setting a Maximum Bid:** With Bid Cap bidding, advertisers specify the maximum amount they are willing to pay for each ad impression or click. This maximum bid is determined by the advertiser and represents the upper limit of what they are willing to spend for their desired outcome.
2. **Automatic Bid Optimization:** Facebook's algorithm automatically adjusts bids in real-time to help advertisers achieve the desired outcomes at or below the specified Bid Cap. The algorithm optimizes bids based on factors such as audience engagement, ad relevance, and competition in the auction.
3. **Budget Control:** Advertisers also set a daily or lifetime budget for their campaign, which helps control overall advertising costs. The Bid Cap ensures that advertisers do not exceed their maximum bid limit, helping them maintain control over their advertising expenses.
4. **Campaign Objective Alignment:** Bid Cap bidding works best when aligned with specific campaign objectives, such as brand awareness, traffic, conversions, or app installs. Advertisers specify the optimization event they want to optimize for, and Facebook's algorithm adjusts bids accordingly to achieve the desired results at or below the Bid Cap.
5. **Performance Monitoring:** It's important for advertisers to monitor the performance of their ads regularly when using the Bid Cap bidding strategy. They should track key metrics such as cost per result, conversion rate, and return on ad spend (ROAS) to assess the effectiveness of their campaign and make any necessary adjustments.
6. **Learning Phase:** Like other bidding strategies, Bid Cap bidding may enter a learning phase when first implemented or when significant changes are made to the campaign. During this phase, Facebook's algorithm gathers data and adjusts bidding strategies to optimize performance. Advertisers may see fluctuations in performance until the algorithm stabilizes.

Overall, Bid Cap bidding provides advertisers with a way to control their advertising costs while still aiming to achieve their campaign objectives. By setting a maximum bid limit, advertisers can ensure that they are getting the most value from their ad spend while staying within their budget constraints.

- *Target Cost*

Target Cost bidding allows you to set a desired cost per optimization event, such as cost per lead or cost per purchase. Facebook will aim to achieve the specified cost while maximizing the number of results.

This bidding strategy is suitable for you who have a specific target cost in mind for your optimization events and want to maintain consistent spending efficiency.

Here's how Target Cost bidding works:

1. **Setting a Desired Cost:** With Target Cost bidding, advertisers specify the average cost they are willing to pay for each optimization event, such as link clicks, conversions, or app installs. This desired cost per result is defined by the advertiser and represents the target cost they aim to achieve.
2. **Automatic Bid Adjustment:** Facebook's algorithm automatically adjusts bids in real-time to help advertisers achieve the specified Target Cost. The algorithm optimizes bids based on factors such as audience engagement, ad relevance, and competition in the auction to reach the desired cost per result.
3. **Budget Control:** Advertisers also set a daily or lifetime budget for their campaign, which helps control overall advertising costs. The Target Cost bidding strategy ensures that advertisers do not exceed their desired cost per result, helping them maintain control over their advertising expenses.
4. **Campaign Objective Alignment:** Target Cost bidding works best when aligned with specific campaign objectives, such as conversions, app installs, or lead generation. Advertisers specify the optimization event they want to optimize for, and Facebook's algorithm adjusts bids accordingly to achieve the desired results at the target cost.
5. **Performance Monitoring:** It's important for advertisers to monitor the performance of their ads regularly when using the Target Cost bidding strategy. They should track key metrics such as cost per result, conversion rate, and return on ad spend (ROAS) to assess the effectiveness of their campaign and make any necessary adjustments.
6. **Learning Phase:** As with other bidding strategies, Target Cost bidding may enter a learning phase when first implemented or when significant changes are made to the campaign. During this phase, Facebook's algorithm gathers data and adjusts bidding strategies to optimize performance. Advertisers may see fluctuations in performance until the algorithm stabilizes.

Overall, Target Cost bidding provides advertisers with a way to achieve a consistent cost per result while still maximizing the volume of results obtained. By setting a desired cost per optimization event, advertisers can ensure that they are getting the most value from their ad spend while reaching their campaign objectives effectively.

- *Bid Strategy Optimization (BSO)*

Bid Strategy Optimization is an advanced bidding strategy that uses machine learning to automatically adjust bids based on real-time auction signals and user behavior. Facebook's algorithm optimizes bids to maximize campaign performance while achieving the advertiser's specified campaign objectives.

This bidding strategy is suitable for you who want to leverage Facebook's advanced optimization capabilities to achieve specific business goals, such as maximizing conversions or return on ad spend (ROAS).

Bid strategy optimization refers to the process of fine-tuning bidding strategies within Facebook Ads Manager to achieve optimal performance for your advertising campaigns. This optimization involves adjusting various bidding parameters and settings to maximize the efficiency and effectiveness of your ad spend. Here's how bid strategy optimization works:

1. **Campaign Objectives Alignment:** The first step in bid strategy optimization is to ensure that your bidding strategy aligns with your campaign objectives. Facebook offers different bidding strategies tailored to specific objectives, such as conversions, app installs, traffic, or brand awareness. Choose the bidding strategy that best aligns with your campaign goals.
2. **Bid Amount Adjustment:** Depending on your campaign objectives and budget constraints, you may need to adjust your bid amounts. For example, if you're using a bid cap strategy, you can set a maximum bid limit for each ad placement. Similarly, if you're using a target cost or lowest cost strategy, you can adjust the target cost or bid amount to optimize performance.
3. **Budget Allocation:** Allocate your campaign budget strategically across different ad sets and audiences based on their performance and potential for achieving your objectives. Monitor the performance of each ad set closely and reallocate budget to

those with the highest return on investment (ROI) or potential for achieving your goals.

4. **Audience Targeting Optimization:** Refine your audience targeting to reach the most relevant audience segments for your campaign. Use Facebook's audience targeting options, such as demographics, interests, behaviors, and custom audiences, to target users who are most likely to engage with your ads and take the desired action.

5. **Ad Creative Optimization:** Optimize your ad creative elements, including ad copy, images, videos, and calls-to-action, to maximize engagement and conversion rates. Test different creative variations and messaging to identify the most effective combinations for your target audience.

6. **Performance Monitoring and Iteration:** Continuously monitor the performance of your ad campaigns and make adjustments based on real-time data and insights. Analyze key performance metrics such as click-through rate (CTR), conversion rate, cost per conversion, return on ad spend (ROAS), and overall campaign performance to identify areas for optimization.

7. **A/B Testing:** Conduct A/B tests to compare different bidding strategies, ad creatives, audience segments, and other variables to determine the most effective approach for achieving your objectives. Test one variable at a time to isolate its impact on performance and make data-driven decisions.

8. **Experimentation and Innovation:** Stay informed about the latest trends, features, and best practices in Facebook advertising, and be open to experimenting with new bidding strategies and tactics. Innovation and experimentation are key to staying ahead of the competition and continuously improving your campaign performance.

By implementing these bid strategy optimization techniques, you can maximize the effectiveness of your Facebook advertising campaigns and achieve better results within your budget constraints. Remember to monitor performance regularly, iterate based on insights, and adapt your strategies to evolving market conditions and audience preferences.

- *Value-Based Bidding*

Value-Based Bidding allows you to optimize bids based on the predicted value of specific conversion events, such as purchases or leads.
you can assign different values to different conversion events and let Facebook's algorithm adjust bids to maximize overall campaign value.

Here's how value-based bidding works and why it's important:

1. **Optimizing for Value:** With value-based bidding, advertisers specify a desired return on ad spend (ROAS) or target cost per acquisition (CPA) based on the value generated from each conversion. Instead of simply maximizing the number of conversions or minimizing the cost per conversion, the bidding algorithm aims to maximize the total value generated from the campaign.

2. **Tracking Customer Actions:** To implement value-based bidding, advertisers need to track customer actions and assign a value to each conversion event. This can include purchases, sign-ups, app installs, or other valuable actions that contribute to the advertiser's business objectives. By tracking the value of each conversion, advertisers can determine the optimal bid amount to maximize return on investment (ROI).

3. **Dynamic Bidding Adjustments:** Facebook's bidding algorithm dynamically adjusts bids in real-time based on the expected value of each ad impression. The algorithm considers factors such as historical performance, audience behavior, and predicted conversion value to determine the optimal bid amount for each ad placement. This allows advertisers to efficiently allocate their budget to the highest-value opportunities.

4. **Flexible Optimization Goals:** Value-based bidding offers flexibility in optimization goals, allowing advertisers to prioritize different metrics based on their business objectives. For example, advertisers can optimize for maximum revenue, maximum profit margin, or maximum customer lifetime value, depending on their strategic priorities and financial goals.

5. **Performance Monitoring and Iteration:** As with any bidding strategy, it's essential for advertisers to monitor the performance of their value-based bidding campaigns closely and make adjustments as needed. Analyze key metrics such as ROAS, CPA, conversion rate, and overall campaign performance to identify areas for optimization and refinement.

6. **Long-Term Value Generation:** Value-based bidding helps advertisers focus on generating long-term value from their ad campaigns rather than just short-term gains. By optimizing for the most valuable customer actions, advertisers can maximize the lifetime value of their customers and drive sustainable business growth over time.

Overall, value-based bidding is a powerful strategy for advertisers looking to maximize the return on their advertising investment and drive meaningful business outcomes. By prioritizing value generation over simple cost metrics, advertisers can unlock new opportunities for growth and profitability in their Facebook advertising campaigns.

This bidding strategy is suitable for you who want to prioritize high-value conversions and allocate budget more efficiently based on the expected return from each conversion event.

Each bidding strategy offers unique advantages and may be suitable for different campaign objectives and budget considerations. you should carefully consider your goals and target audience when selecting the most appropriate bidding strategy for your Facebook Ads campaigns. Additionally, ongoing monitoring and optimization are essential to ensure that the chosen bidding strategy delivers the desired results effectively.

4.2. Setting an appropriate budget for your campaigns

Setting an appropriate budget for your Facebook Ads campaigns requires careful consideration of your marketing objectives, target audience, competition, and overall business goals. Here are some steps to help you determine an appropriate budget for your campaigns:

Define Your Objectives: Start by clearly defining your campaign objectives. Are you looking to increase brand awareness, drive website traffic, generate leads, or increase sales? Your budget should align with your objectives and the desired outcomes of your campaigns.

Understand Your Audience: Understand your target audience and your behaviors on Facebook. Consider factors such as demographics, interests, purchasing behavior, and geographical location. The size and characteristics of your audience can influence your budget allocation.

Research Your Competition: Research your competitors' advertising efforts on Facebook. Look at the types of ads they are running, the messaging they use, and your level of investment. This can give you insights into industry benchmarks and help you determine a competitive budget.

Set Realistic Goals: Set realistic and achievable goals for your campaigns. Consider factors such as the size of your target audience, the level of competition in your industry, and your historical performance data. Set specific targets for key performance indicators (KPIs) such as reach, engagement, conversions, and return on ad spend (ROAS).

Calculate Estimated Costs: Use Facebook's Ad Manager tool to estimate the potential costs of running your campaigns. Facebook provides estimates for metrics such as reach, impressions, clicks, and conversions based on your targeting options, bid strategy, and budget.

Consider Your Resources: Evaluate your available resources, including budget, time, and manpower. Determine how much you can realistically invest in advertising without stretching your resources too thin. Consider factors such as creative production costs, ad management fees, and ongoing optimization efforts.

Start Small and Scale: If you're new to Facebook Ads or testing a new campaign, start with a smaller budget and scale up gradually based on performance. This allows you to minimize risk and test different strategies before committing larger budgets.

Monitor and Adjust: Regularly monitor the performance of your campaigns and adjust your budget accordingly. Analyze key metrics such as click-through rate (CTR), conversion rate, cost per conversion, and ROAS to determine the effectiveness of your advertising efforts. Allocate more budget to top-performing campaigns and adjust or pause underperforming ones.

Allocate Budget Across Campaigns: If you're running multiple campaigns simultaneously, allocate your budget strategically based on the priority of each campaign and your respective objectives. Consider factors such as campaign duration, audience size, and expected results when dividing your budget across campaigns.

Optimize Over Time: Continuously optimize your campaigns based on performance data and insights. Experiment with different targeting options, ad creatives, and bidding strategies to improve results and maximize your return on investment.

By following these steps and taking a strategic approach to budgeting, you can set an appropriate budget for your Facebook Ads campaigns that aligns with your objectives, resources, and target audience, ultimately driving meaningful results for your business.

4.3. Optimizing cost per action (CPA) and return on investment (ROI)

Optimizing cost per action (CPA) and return on investment (ROI) are essential for ensuring the efficiency and effectiveness of your Facebook Ads campaigns. Here are some strategies to optimize CPA and ROI:

- Set Clear Objectives: Define specific conversion actions that you want users to take, such as purchases, sign-ups, or app installs. Establish clear targets for your CPA and ROI based on your campaign objectives and business goals.

- Track Conversions: Implement conversion tracking using the Facebook pixel or other tracking tools to measure the actions users take after clicking on your ads. Track key conversion metrics such as purchases, leads, registrations, or downloads to understand the effectiveness of your campaigns.

- Optimize Targeting: Refine your audience targeting to reach users who are most likely to convert. Use Facebook's targeting options to target users based on demographics, interests, behaviors, and custom audiences. Experiment with different audience segments to identify high-value audiences with lower CPAs.

- Improve Ad Relevance: Create compelling ad creatives that resonate with your target audience and clearly communicate the value proposition of your products or services. Use high-quality images or videos, persuasive ad copy, and strong calls-to-action (CTAs) to encourage users to take action.

- Test Ad Creative and Copy: A/B test different ad creatives, headlines, and copy variations to identify which elements drive the highest conversion rates and ROI. Test different messaging, visuals, offers, and CTAs to optimize ad performance and minimize CPA.

- Optimize Landing Pages: Ensure that your landing pages are optimized for conversions and provide a seamless user experience. Make sure your landing pages load quickly, have clear and compelling messaging, and feature prominent CTAs that encourage users to take action.

- Adjust Bidding Strategies: Experiment with different bidding strategies such as lowest cost, target cost, or bid cap to optimize your CPA and ROI. Monitor the performance of your campaigns and adjust your bidding strategy based on performance data and objectives.

- Monitor Performance Metrics: Regularly monitor key performance metrics such as CPA, conversion rate, click-through rate (CTR), and ROI. Use performance data to identify trends, opportunities, and areas for improvement. Allocate more budget to top-performing campaigns and adjust or pause underperforming ones.

- Optimize Ad Frequency: Monitor ad frequency to avoid ad fatigue and ensure that users are not being bombarded with the same ads too frequently. Rotate ad creatives and refresh your ad content regularly to maintain user interest and engagement.

- Focus on Lifetime Value (LTV): Consider the lifetime value of customers when evaluating the ROI of your campaigns. Focus on acquiring high-value customers who are likely to make repeat purchases or engage with your brand over the long term, rather than solely optimizing for immediate conversions.

By implementing these strategies and continuously optimizing your campaigns based on performance data and insights, you can effectively optimize your cost per action (CPA) and maximize return on investment (ROI) from your Facebook Ads campaigns.

Chapter 5: Campaign Management and Optimization

5.1. Monitoring campaign performance in real-time

Monitoring campaign performance in real-time is crucial for making timely adjustments and maximizing the effectiveness of your Facebook Ads campaigns. Here's how you can monitor your campaign performance in real-time:

- *Use Facebook Ads Manager*

Access Facebook Ads Manager to monitor your campaigns, ad sets, and individual ads in real-time. Ads Manager provides a comprehensive overview of key performance metrics such as impressions, reach, clicks, conversions, and ad spend.

To set up custom reports in Facebook Ads Manager, follow these steps:
1. **Access Ads Manager:** Log in to your Facebook account and navigate to Ads Manager. You can access Ads Manager by clicking on the drop-down arrow in the top-right corner of the Facebook homepage and selecting "Ads Manager," or by visiting business.facebook.com/adsmanager directly.
2. **Navigate to Reports:** In Ads Manager, click on the "Reports" tab located in the sidebar menu on the left-hand side of the screen. This will take you to the Reports section where you can create and manage custom reports.
3. **Create a New Report:** Click on the "Create" button to start creating a new custom report. You'll be prompted to choose the type of report you want to create.
4. **Choose Reporting Type:** Facebook Ads Manager offers several reporting options, including Performance, Delivery, and Export Data. Select the type of report that best suits your needs.
5. **Select Metrics:** Once you've chosen the reporting type, you can select the specific metrics and key performance indicators (KPIs) you want to include in your report. You can choose from a wide range of metrics such as reach, impressions, clicks, conversions, cost per result, and more.
6. **Apply Filters:** Optionally, you can apply filters to narrow down the data included in your report. Filters allow you to segment your data based on specific criteria such as date range, campaign objectives, ad sets, ads, demographics, and more.

7. **Customize Columns:** Customize the columns in your report to display the metrics and dimensions that are most relevant to your analysis. You can add, remove, or rearrange columns to tailor the report to your preferences.
8. **Save and Name Your Report:** Once you've configured your report settings, give your report a name and click on the "Save" button to save it for future use. You can also choose to schedule the report to run automatically at specific intervals.
9. **View and Export Report:** After saving your report, you can view it directly in Ads Manager. You can also export the report data to a CSV or Excel file for further analysis or sharing with stakeholders.
10. **Manage and Edit Reports:** You can manage and edit your custom reports at any time by navigating to the Reports section in Ads Manager. Here, you can view your saved reports, make changes to existing reports, or delete reports that are no longer needed.

By setting up custom reports in Facebook Ads Manager, you can track and analyze the performance of your advertising campaigns more effectively, gain valuable insights, and make data-driven decisions to optimize your advertising strategies.

- *Customize Performance Dashboards*

Customize your Ads Manager dashboard to display the metrics most relevant to your campaign objectives. Create custom reports and dashboards to track performance metrics specific to your goals, such as conversion rate, cost per conversion, return on ad spend (ROAS), and more.

To customize performance dashboards in Facebook Ads Manager, follow these steps:

1. **Access Ads Manager:** Log in to your Facebook account and navigate to Ads Manager. You can access Ads Manager by clicking on the drop-down arrow in the top-right corner of the Facebook homepage and selecting "Ads Manager," or by visiting business.facebook.com/adsmanager directly.
2. **Navigate to Performance Dashboard:** In Ads Manager, click on the "Performance" tab located in the sidebar menu on the left-hand side of the screen. This will take you to the Performance Dashboard where you can view various metrics and key performance indicators (KPIs) for your advertising campaigns.

3. **Customize Dashboard:** Once you're on the Performance Dashboard, you'll see a range of pre-built dashboard cards displaying different metrics such as reach, impressions, clicks, conversions, and more. To customize the dashboard, click on the "Customize" button located at the top-right corner of the dashboard.
4. **Add or Remove Cards:** In the customization menu, you can add new cards to the dashboard by clicking on the "Add Card" button. This will open a list of available metrics and KPIs that you can choose from to add to your dashboard. You can also remove existing cards from the dashboard by clicking on the "X" icon next to the card you want to remove.
5. **Organize Cards:** You can rearrange the order of cards on the dashboard by clicking and dragging them to the desired position. This allows you to prioritize the metrics that are most important to you and your advertising goals.
6. **Adjust Card Settings:** Each card on the dashboard comes with customizable settings that allow you to further tailor the display of data. Click on the settings icon (usually represented by three dots) on a card to access its settings menu. Here, you can adjust settings such as date range, comparison periods, breakdowns, and more.
7. **Save Customizations:** Once you've customized your dashboard to your liking, click on the "Save" button to save your changes. You can choose to save your customizations as a new dashboard or overwrite an existing dashboard.
8. **View Custom Dashboard:** After saving your customizations, you can easily access your custom dashboard from the Performance tab in Ads Manager. Your custom dashboard will display the metrics and KPIs that you selected, allowing you to monitor the performance of your advertising campaigns more effectively.

By customizing performance dashboards in Facebook Ads Manager, you can create personalized views of your advertising data that are tailored to your specific needs and objectives. This allows you to gain deeper insights into the performance of your campaigns and make informed decisions to optimize your advertising strategies.

- *Set Up Automated Alerts*

Configure automated alerts and notifications within Ads Manager to receive real-time updates on campaign performance. Set thresholds for key metrics such as CTR, CPA, or budget spend, and receive alerts when performance deviates from your specified targets.

To set up automated alerts in Facebook Ads Manager to monitor the performance of your advertising campaigns, follow these steps:

1. **Access Ads Manager:** Log in to your Facebook account and navigate to Ads Manager. You can access Ads Manager by clicking on the drop-down arrow in the top-right corner of the Facebook homepage and selecting "Ads Manager," or by visiting business.facebook.com/adsmanager directly.

2. **Navigate to Alerts:** In Ads Manager, click on the "Alerts" tab located in the sidebar menu on the left-hand side of the screen. This will take you to the Alerts section where you can create and manage automated alerts for your campaigns.

3. **Create New Alert:** Click on the "Create Alert" button to start setting up a new automated alert. You'll be prompted to choose the criteria for the alert.

4. **Choose Alert Conditions:** Specify the conditions that will trigger the alert. You can set alerts based on various metrics such as reach, impressions, clicks, conversions, cost, and more. For example, you can set an alert to notify you when the cost per conversion exceeds a certain threshold.

5. **Set Thresholds:** Define the thresholds for the alert conditions. This includes specifying the specific values or ranges that will trigger the alert. For example, you can set a threshold for the cost per conversion to be greater than $10.

6. **Select Delivery Method:** Choose how you want to receive the alert notifications. You can opt to receive alerts via email, Facebook notification, or both.

7. **Name and Save Alert:** Give your alert a descriptive name that reflects the conditions it monitors. Once you've configured the alert settings, click on the "Save" button to save the alert.

8. **Review and Manage Alerts:** After saving the alert, you'll see it listed in the Alerts section of Ads Manager. Here, you can review and manage all your alerts. You can edit or delete existing alerts, as well as create new alerts as needed.

9. **Monitor Alert Notifications:** Once your alerts are set up, you'll receive notifications whenever the specified conditions are met. This allows you to stay informed about the performance of your advertising campaigns and take action promptly if any issues arise.

By setting up automated alerts in Facebook Ads Manager, you can proactively monitor the performance of your campaigns and quickly identify any anomalies or issues that require attention. This helps you optimize your advertising strategies and maximize the effectiveness of your campaigns.

- *Monitor Audience Insights*

Utilize Facebook's Audience Insights tool to gain valuable insights into your target audience's demographics, interests, behaviors, and engagement patterns. Monitor audience insights in real-time to identify trends, preferences, and opportunities for optimization.

To monitor audience insights in Facebook Ads Manager, follow these steps:
1. **Access Ads Manager:** Log in to your Facebook account and navigate to Ads Manager. You can access Ads Manager by clicking on the drop-down arrow in the top-right corner of the Facebook homepage and selecting "Ads Manager," or by visiting business.facebook.com/adsmanager directly.
2. **Navigate to Audience Insights:** In Ads Manager, click on the "Audience Insights" tab located in the sidebar menu on the left-hand side of the screen. This will take you to the Audience Insights tool where you can analyze data about your target audience.
3. **Choose Audience:** By default, Audience Insights will show you insights about the general Facebook audience. To analyze insights about a specific audience segment, click on the "Everyone on Facebook" dropdown menu at the top of the page and select the audience you want to analyze. You can choose from options such as people connected to your Page, a custom audience, or people in a specific location or demographic.
4. **Explore Demographics:** In the Audience Insights tool, you can explore various demographic data about your selected audience, including age, gender, location, language, education level, relationship status, and more. Use the tabs on the left-hand side of the page to navigate between different categories of insights.
5. **Analyze Page Likes:** The "Page Likes" tab allows you to see the top Pages that people in your selected audience segment like on Facebook. This can help you understand their interests and preferences, as well as identify potential competitors or complementary brands.
6. **View Location and Activity:** The "Location" and "Activity" tabs provide insights into where your audience is located geographically and how active they are on Facebook (e.g., frequency of interactions, devices used).
7. **Explore Purchase Behavior:** If applicable, you can use the "Purchase Behavior" tab to analyze insights related to the online purchasing behavior of your audience, such as purchase activity, device usage for purchases, and spending habits.

8. **Review Insights and Take Action:** Use the data and insights provided in Audience Insights to inform your advertising strategies and optimize your campaigns. Identify trends, preferences, and opportunities within your target audience and adjust your targeting, messaging, and creative accordingly.
9. **Save and Export Data:** If desired, you can save or export the data from Audience Insights for further analysis or sharing with stakeholders. Use the buttons at the top of the page to save the audience or export the data to a CSV file.
10. **Monitor Changes Over Time:** Regularly monitor audience insights to track changes in your audience demographics, behavior, and preferences over time. This will help you stay informed and adapt your strategies to evolving audience dynamics.

By monitoring audience insights in Facebook Ads Manager, you can gain valuable information about your target audience, understand their preferences and behavior, and make data-driven decisions to improve the effectiveness of your advertising campaigns.

- *Track Conversions with the Facebook Pixel*

Implement the Facebook pixel on your website to track conversions and user interactions in real-time. Monitor conversion events such as purchases, sign-ups, or downloads as they occur, and analyze the performance of different audience segments and ad creatives.

To track conversions with the Facebook Pixel, follow these steps:
1. **Set Up the Facebook Pixel:** If you haven't already, create and install the Facebook Pixel on your website. You can do this by accessing Events Manager in your Facebook Business Manager account, selecting "Pixels" from the menu, and following the instructions to set up and install the pixel code on your website.
2. **Define Conversion Events:** Decide which actions or events on your website you want to track as conversions. Common conversion events include purchases, sign-ups, form submissions, and page views.
3. **Add Pixel Events Code:** For each conversion event you want to track, add the corresponding pixel event code to the relevant pages on your website. You can use standard events provided by Facebook (e.g., Purchase, Add to Cart, Complete Registration) or create custom events tailored to your specific goals.
4. **Test Pixel Events:** Once you've added the pixel events code to your website, test them to ensure they are tracking conversions correctly. Use Facebook's Event Setup

Tool or the Pixel Helper browser extension to verify that the pixel is firing correctly and capturing the desired events.

5. **Set Up Custom Conversions:** In Facebook Ads Manager, navigate to the "Events Manager" and click on "Aggregated Event Measurement." Here, you can set up custom conversions by selecting the pixel events you want to track as conversions and defining conversion rules based on URL parameters or other criteria.

6. **Create Conversion-Based Campaigns:** When creating ad campaigns in Facebook Ads Manager, choose the "Conversions" objective to optimize your campaigns for the conversion events you've defined. This allows Facebook to automatically deliver your ads to people most likely to take the desired actions on your website.

7. **Monitor Conversion Tracking:** After launching your campaigns, monitor conversion tracking in Ads Manager to evaluate their performance. Track key metrics such as conversion rate, cost per conversion, and return on ad spend (ROAS) to assess the effectiveness of your advertising efforts.

8. **Optimize Campaigns:** Use the conversion data collected by the Facebook Pixel to optimize your ad campaigns. Adjust targeting, bidding, ad creative, and other campaign elements based on insights gained from conversion tracking to improve campaign performance and maximize results.

9. **Iterate and Improve:** Continuously analyze conversion data and iterate on your campaigns to improve results over time. Test different strategies, experiment with new audience segments, and refine your approach based on the insights gathered from conversion tracking.

By tracking conversions with the Facebook Pixel, you can gain valuable insights into the effectiveness of your advertising campaigns, optimize your targeting and messaging to drive more conversions, and ultimately achieve your business goals.

Monitor Ad Auctions and Bidding

Keep an eye on ad auctions and bidding dynamics in real-time to ensure that your ads are competing effectively for placement. Monitor bid strategies, auction insights, and competitor activity to optimize your bidding strategy and maximize ad performance.

Monitoring ad auctions and bidding in Facebook Ads Manager is essential for optimizing your campaigns and maximizing their performance. Here's how to do it:

1. **Access Ads Manager:** Log in to your Facebook account and navigate to Ads Manager.
2. **Select Campaigns:** From the Ads Manager dashboard, click on the "Campaigns" tab to view a list of your active campaigns.
3. **Review Ad Sets:** Click on the campaign that you want to monitor ad auctions and bidding for. This will expand to show all ad sets within that campaign.
4. **Analyze Ad Set Performance:** Review the performance of each ad set within the campaign. Look at key metrics such as reach, impressions, clicks, and conversions to assess how each ad set is performing.
5. **Check Bidding Strategies:** Evaluate the bidding strategy used for each ad set. Facebook offers various bidding strategies such as lowest cost, target cost, bid cap, and cost cap. Ensure that the bidding strategy aligns with your campaign objectives and budget constraints.
6. **Monitor Bid Amounts:** Keep an eye on the bid amounts set for each ad set. Facebook automatically optimizes bids to help you reach your campaign objectives while staying within your budget. If necessary, adjust bid amounts to ensure competitiveness in the ad auctions.
7. **Assess Ad Auction Insights:** Utilize Facebook's auction insights to gain visibility into how your ads are performing in auctions compared to other advertisers. Look for opportunities to improve your ad positioning and competitiveness in the auctions.
8. **Optimize Targeting:** Review the targeting criteria used for each ad set. Ensure that your targeting is relevant to your audience and aligned with your campaign objectives. Consider making adjustments to targeting parameters based on audience insights and performance data.
9. **Experiment with Ad Creative:** Test different ad creatives to see how they impact ad performance and bidding in auctions. Experiment with variations in images, videos, ad copy, and calls-to-action to find the most effective combinations.
10. **Adjust Campaign Settings:** Based on your analysis of ad auctions and bidding, make adjustments to campaign settings as needed. This could include reallocating budgets, pausing underperforming ad sets, or scaling up successful ones.
11. **Monitor and Iterate:** Continuously monitor the performance of your campaigns and iterate on your strategies based on the insights gained. Test new bidding strategies, refine targeting, and optimize ad creative to improve overall campaign effectiveness over time.

By closely monitoring ad auctions and bidding in Facebook Ads Manager, you can make informed decisions to optimize your campaigns, drive better results, and achieve your advertising objectives.

Test and Iterate

Continuously test different ad creatives, targeting options, ad formats, and bidding strategies to identify what resonates best with your audience. Monitor test results in real-time and iterate on your campaigns based on performance data to improve results over time.

Testing and iterating are crucial aspects of optimizing Facebook ad campaigns. Here's how to effectively test and iterate your campaigns:

1. **Define Testing Objectives:** Clearly define your testing objectives before conducting any experiments. Determine what specific elements of your campaigns you want to test and what metrics you'll use to measure success.
2. **Identify Test Variables:** Identify the variables you want to test, which may include ad creatives (images, videos, ad copy), targeting options (demographics, interests, behaviors), ad formats (carousel ads, single image ads, video ads), and bidding strategies (lowest cost, target cost, bid cap).
3. **Create Test Groups:** Divide your audience into test groups based on the variables you want to test. For example, create separate ad sets with different ad creatives or targeting options to compare their performance.
4. **Set Up A/B Tests:** Use Facebook's A/B testing feature to compare the performance of different elements within your campaigns. Set up experiments to test one variable at a time, keeping all other factors constant to isolate the impact of each variable.
5. **Run Experiments:** Launch your A/B tests and let them run for a sufficient period to gather meaningful data. Monitor the performance of each test group closely, tracking key metrics such as click-through rate (CTR), conversion rate, cost per conversion, and return on ad spend (ROAS).
6. **Analyze Results:** After the experiments have run for an appropriate duration, analyze the results to determine which variations performed best. Look for statistically significant differences in performance between test groups and identify trends or patterns in the data.

7. **Draw Insights:** Use the insights gained from your experiments to inform your future campaign optimization efforts. Identify which ad creatives, targeting options, ad formats, and bidding strategies resonate best with your audience and drive the highest return on investment (ROI).
8. **Iterate and Optimize:** Based on your analysis of the test results, make data-driven decisions to optimize your campaigns. Implement the winning variations across your campaigns and continue to iterate by testing new hypotheses and refining your strategies over time.
9. **Scale Up Successful Strategies:** Once you've identified winning strategies through testing, scale up your successful campaigns to reach a larger audience and maximize your results. Allocate more budget to high-performing ad sets and replicate successful elements across new campaigns.
10. **Continuous Testing:** Testing and iterating should be an ongoing process in your Facebook advertising strategy. Continuously test new ideas, explore different tactics, and adapt to changes in your audience's behavior to stay ahead of the competition and drive continuous improvement in your campaigns.

By systematically testing and iterating on your Facebook ad campaigns, you can identify the most effective strategies for reaching and engaging your target audience, ultimately driving better results and achieving your advertising goals.

Stay Agile and Responsive: Be prepared to make quick adjustments to your campaigns based on real-time performance data and insights. Allocate budget to top-performing campaigns, adjust targeting parameters, or update ad creatives as needed to optimize performance and achieve your goals.

By monitoring campaign performance in real-time and taking proactive steps to optimize your campaigns based on data-driven insights, you can maximize the effectiveness of your Facebook Ads campaigns and achieve better results.

5.2 A/B testing to improve results

A/B testing is a powerful technique used in marketing to compare two versions of a campaign element and determine which one performs better. Here's how you can use A/B testing to improve the results of your Facebook Ads campaigns:

- ✓ Identify Test Variables: Determine which elements of your ad campaign you want to test. This could include ad creative (images, videos, copy), ad format (single image, carousel, slideshow), targeting options (audience demographics, interests, behaviors), bidding strategies, or landing page design.

- ✓ Set Clear Hypotheses: Establish clear hypotheses for your A/B tests. What specific outcome are you expecting to see? For example, you might hypothesize that a video ad will outperform a static image ad in terms of engagement or that targeting a specific audience segment will lead to higher conversion rates.

- ✓ Split Test Groups: Divide your audience into two or more test groups and allocate a portion of your budget to each group. Ensure that the test groups are similar in size and composition to obtain accurate and meaningful results.

- ✓ Create Test Variations: Develop different variations of the element you're testing, making only one change at a time. For example, if you're testing ad creative, create two versions of the ad with different images or headlines while keeping other elements constant.

- ✓ Run Experiments Concurrently: Run your A/B tests concurrently to minimize the impact of external factors and ensure that the results are comparable. Launch both test variations simultaneously and monitor your performance in real-time using Facebook Ads Manager.

- ✓ Measure Key Metrics: Track key performance metrics for each test variation, such as click-through rate (CTR), conversion rate, cost per conversion, return on ad spend

(ROAS), or engagement rate. Use Facebook's built-in analytics tools to monitor performance and gather data.

- ✓ Analyze Results: Once your A/B test has concluded, analyze the results to determine which variation performed better against your established metrics. Look for statistically significant differences in performance between the test variations.

- ✓ Draw Conclusions and Take Action: Based on the results of your A/B test, draw conclusions about which variation was more effective in achieving your campaign objectives. Implement the winning variation and make adjustments to your campaigns accordingly.

- ✓ Iterate and Repeat: A/B testing is an ongoing process of iteration and optimization. Use the insights gained from your tests to inform future campaign decisions and continue refining your strategies over time.

- ✓ Document Learnings: Document the results of your A/B tests, including what worked well and what didn't, to inform your future marketing efforts. Use these learnings to refine your overall marketing strategy and improve the effectiveness of your Facebook Ads campaigns.

By systematically conducting A/B tests and leveraging the insights gained, you can optimize your Facebook Ads campaigns, improve results, and ultimately drive better outcomes for your business.

5.3. Adjusting and optimizing campaigns for better outcomes

Adjusting and optimizing campaigns is a critical process for achieving better outcomes with your Facebook Ads. Here's a step-by-step guide on how to adjust and optimize your campaigns effectively:

- Analyze Performance Metrics: Start by analyzing the performance metrics of your campaigns using Facebook Ads Manager or other analytics tools. Look at key metrics such as click-through rate (CTR), conversion rate, cost per conversion, return on ad spend (ROAS), and overall campaign performance.

- Identify Underperforming Elements: Identify the elements of your campaigns that are underperforming or not meeting your objectives. This could include ad creative, targeting options, bidding strategies, ad placements, or audience segments.

- Diagnose Issues: Diagnose the root causes of underperformance by examining the data and identifying patterns or trends. Look for areas where performance is lagging behind expectations and determine what factors may be contributing to the problem.

- Make Data-Driven Adjustments: Based on your analysis, make data-driven adjustments to your campaigns to address the identified issues and improve performance. This could involve tweaking ad creative, refining audience targeting, adjusting bidding strategies, or optimizing ad placements.

- Experiment with A/B Testing: Conduct A/B tests to compare different variations of campaign elements and identify what resonates best with your audience. Test different ad creatives, headlines, copy variations, targeting options, or bidding strategies to optimize performance.

- Optimize Budget Allocation: Review your budget allocation across campaigns, ad sets, and individual ads to ensure optimal distribution of resources. Allocate more budget to top-performing campaigns or ad sets while scaling back spending on underperforming ones.

- Monitor Competitor Activity: Keep an eye on competitor activity and industry trends to stay informed about changes in the competitive landscape. Identify emerging opportunities or areas where competitors may be gaining an advantage and adjust your strategies accordingly.

- Stay Agile and Responsive: Be prepared to make quick adjustments to your campaigns based on real-time performance data and market conditions. Monitor campaign performance closely and be ready to pivot or iterate on your strategies as needed to stay ahead of the curve.

- Continuously Test and Iterate: Maintain a culture of continuous testing and iteration to drive ongoing improvement in your campaigns. Experiment with new ideas, strategies, and tactics to keep your campaigns fresh and responsive to changing audience preferences.

- Document Learnings: Document the outcomes of your adjustments and optimizations, including what worked well and what didn't. Use these learnings to inform future campaign decisions and refine your overall marketing strategy over time.

By following these steps and adopting a proactive approach to adjusting and optimizing your campaigns, you can drive better outcomes and maximize the effectiveness of your Facebook Ads efforts.

Chapter 6: Case Studies and Practical Examples

6.1 Examples of successful Facebook Ads campaigns

Here are some examples of successful Facebook Ads campaigns focused on driving sales:

- *Amazon's Prime Day Sale*

Amazon's Prime Day sale is one of the largest online shopping events globally, and Facebook Ads play a significant role in promoting it. Amazon runs targeted ad campaigns on Facebook to reach its massive audience base and drive traffic to its Prime Day deals. The ads highlight exclusive discounts, limited-time offers, and popular products to incentivize users to make purchases during the sale period.

- *Target's Holiday Sales Campaign*

Target's holiday sales campaigns leverage Facebook Ads to promote its seasonal promotions and special offers. Target creates ad campaigns featuring holiday-themed visuals, gift ideas, and promotional messaging to entice shoppers to visit its stores or website. The ads often include discounts, free shipping offers, and other incentives to encourage immediate purchase.

- *Sephora's Beauty Insider Sale*

Sephora's Beauty Insider sale is a semi-annual event where members of its loyalty program receive exclusive discounts on beauty products. Sephora promotes the sale through targeted Facebook Ads tailored to different audience segments based on your beauty preferences, purchase history, and membership status. The ads feature enticing visuals of popular beauty products and highlight the limited-time discounts available to Beauty Insider members.

- *Best Buy's Black Friday Deals*

Best Buy's Black Friday ad campaigns on Facebook are highly anticipated by shoppers looking for electronics and tech gadgets at discounted prices. Best Buy uses Facebook Ads to showcase its Black Friday doorbuster deals, early access offers, and online-exclusive discounts. The ads drive traffic to Best Buy's website or stores, where customers can take advantage of the limited-time savings.

- *Zara's End-of-Season Clearance Sale*

Zara's end-of-season clearance sale is promoted through targeted Facebook Ads featuring discounted clothing and accessories. Zara uses dynamic ads to retarget users who have previously visited its website or engaged with its products. The ads showcase clearance items tailored to each user's browsing history or preferences, driving traffic back to the website and encouraging purchases.

- *Airbnb's "Live There" Campaign*

Airbnb launched a campaign called "Live There" to promote unique travel experiences and position itself as more than just a lodging provider. The campaign featured user-generated content showcasing local experiences and activities, encouraging travelers to "live like locals" in destinations around the world. The ads emphasized the value of authentic experiences and personal connections, resonating with Airbnb's target audience of adventurous travelers.

- *Dollar Shave Club's Video Ads*

Dollar Shave Club gained widespread recognition for its humorous and engaging video ads on Facebook. your ads featured quirky humor, catchy slogans, and straightforward messaging to promote your subscription-based razor and grooming products. The ads went viral, generating millions of views and driving significant brand awareness and customer acquisition for Dollar Shave Club.

- *Casper's Carousel Ads*

Casper, a mattress and sleep products company, used carousel ads on Facebook to showcase its product range and highlight key features and benefits. Each carousel card featured a different product image and accompanying text, allowing users to swipe through the ad to learn more. The visually appealing and interactive format helped Casper effectively showcase its product lineup and drive engagement and conversions.

- *Pura Vida Bracelets' User-Generated Content Campaign*

Pura Vida Bracelets leveraged user-generated content (UGC) in its Facebook Ads campaigns to showcase its handmade jewelry and accessories. The company encouraged customers to share photos of themselves wearing Pura Vida products on social media using specific hashtags. Pura Vida then repurposed this UGC in its Facebook ads, featuring real customers and your stories to create authentic and relatable content that resonated with its target audience.

- *Nike's Custom Audience Targeting*

Nike used advanced targeting options on Facebook to reach specific audience segments with personalized ad content. For example, Nike created custom audiences based on users' past purchase behavior, engagement with the brand, or interests in specific sports or activities. By tailoring its ads to different audience segments, Nike was able to deliver more relevant and compelling messages, driving higher engagement and conversions.

6.2. Analyzing case studies for applied understanding of discussed concepts

- **Amazon's Prime Day Sale** is a prime example (pun intended!) of a highly successful Facebook Ads campaign focused on driving sales. Here's how Amazon leverages Facebook Ads for its Prime Day event:

Pre-Event Hype: In the weeks leading up to Prime Day, Amazon creates anticipation and excitement through targeted Facebook Ads. These ads tease upcoming deals, highlight exclusive offers for Prime members, and encourage users to mark your calendars for the event.

Promotion of Deals: On Prime Day itself, Amazon launches a barrage of Facebook Ads showcasing its most attractive deals and discounts. These ads feature a wide range of products, from electronics to home goods to fashion, catering to diverse interests and preferences.

Limited-Time Offers: Amazon uses urgency and scarcity tactics in its Facebook Ads by emphasizing limited-time offers and countdown timers. This creates a sense of urgency among users, encouraging them to act quickly to take advantage of the deals before they expire.

Personalized Recommendations: Amazon leverages its extensive customer data to personalize Facebook Ads based on users' browsing history, purchase behavior, and interests. These personalized ads showcase products that are relevant to each user's preferences, increasing the likelihood of conversion.

Cross-Platform Promotion: Amazon extends its Prime Day promotion beyond Facebook to other social media platforms, email marketing, and its own website. This multi-channel approach ensures maximum exposure and engagement with its target audience, driving traffic and sales across various platforms.

Retargeting: Amazon employs retargeting strategies in its Facebook Ads to reach users who have previously visited its website or shown interest in specific products. These ads remind users of items left in your shopping cart, recommend related products, or highlight deals they may have missed, maximizing conversion opportunities.

Post-Event Follow-Up: After Prime Day concludes, Amazon continues to engage with users through follow-up Facebook Ads. These ads may feature post-event promotions, thank-you messages to customers, or reminders to leave reviews for purchased products, fostering long-term customer relationships and loyalty.

Amazon's Prime Day Sale exemplifies how a well-executed Facebook Ads campaign can drive massive sales and engagement by leveraging targeted advertising, personalized recommendations, and strategic promotion tactics.

- **Target's Holiday Sales Campaign** is a stellar example of how the retail giant effectively utilizes Facebook Ads to drive sales during the holiday season. Here's how Target implements its holiday sales campaign on Facebook:

Seasonal Messaging: Target tailors its Facebook Ads with festive and holiday-themed messaging, imagery, and offers to capitalize on the holiday spirit and encourage users to shop for gifts and seasonal essentials.

Promotion of Special Offers: Target promotes its holiday sales and special offers through targeted Facebook Ads. These ads highlight discounts, promotions, and limited-time deals on popular holiday items such as toys, electronics, home goods, and apparel.

Adaptive Targeting: Target utilizes Facebook's advanced targeting capabilities to reach specific audience segments based on demographics, interests, and past purchase behavior. The ads are tailored to appeal to different groups of holiday shoppers, such as parents, tech enthusiasts, or home decorators.

Multi-Channel Promotion: Target integrates its Facebook Ads campaign with other marketing channels, including email marketing, website promotions, and in-store signage. This multi-channel approach ensures consistent messaging and maximizes exposure to target audiences across various touchpoints.

Interactive Content: Target creates engaging and interactive Facebook Ads that encourage user interaction and participation. This may include shoppable posts, interactive quizzes, or holiday-themed contests and giveaways, fostering engagement and driving traffic to Target's online and offline stores.

Gift Inspiration: Target provides gift inspiration and ideas through its Facebook Ads to help users find the perfect presents for your loved ones. The ads showcase curated collections, trending products, and gift guides to simplify the shopping experience and inspire holiday shoppers.

Convenient Shopping Experience: Target emphasizes the convenience of shopping with features like free shipping, curbside pickup, and same-day delivery in its Facebook Ads. This messaging reassures users that they can easily and safely complete your holiday shopping with Target, even amidst the holiday rush.

Post-Purchase Follow-Up: After users make purchases, Target follows up with post-purchase Facebook Ads. These ads may include recommendations for complementary products, invitations to join loyalty programs, or exclusive offers for future purchases, encouraging repeat business and fostering customer loyalty.

Target's Holiday Sales Campaign on Facebook exemplifies how strategic targeting, compelling messaging, and integrated marketing efforts can drive sales and engagement during the busiest shopping season of the year.

- **Best Buy's Black Friday Deals** campaign is a prime example of how the electronics retailer leverages Facebook Ads to drive sales during one of the biggest shopping events of the year. Here's how Best Buy executes its Black Friday campaign on Facebook:

Pre-Event Teasers: Leading up to Black Friday, Best Buy generates anticipation and excitement through targeted Facebook Ads teasing upcoming deals and promotions. These ads build anticipation for the event and encourage users to stay tuned for exclusive offers.

Highlighting Doorbuster Deals: On Black Friday itself, Best Buy showcases its most enticing deals and doorbusters through Facebook Ads. These ads feature popular electronics, gadgets, and appliances at heavily discounted prices, enticing users to shop online or visit Best Buy stores.

Limited-Time Offers: Best Buy creates a sense of urgency in its Facebook Ads by emphasizing limited-time offers and countdown timers. These ads convey the urgency of the Black Friday sale and encourage users to act quickly to secure the best deals before they expire.

Cross-Platform Promotion: Best Buy extends its Black Friday promotion beyond Facebook to other digital channels, including email marketing, website promotions, and mobile apps. This multi-channel approach ensures maximum exposure and engagement with its target audience across various touchpoints.

Personalized Recommendations: Best Buy utilizes data-driven targeting in its Facebook Ads to personalize offers based on users' preferences, past purchase behavior, and interactions with the brand. These personalized ads showcase products that are relevant to each user's interests, increasing the likelihood of conversion.

In-Store and Online Integration: Best Buy seamlessly integrates its online and offline channels in its Black Friday campaign. Facebook Ads drive traffic to both Best Buy's e-commerce website and physical stores, allowing customers to shop in the manner that's most convenient for them.

Post-Purchase Engagement: After Black Friday concludes, Best Buy continues to engage with customers through follow-up Facebook Ads. These ads may feature post-sale promotions, recommendations for related products, or reminders to leave reviews, fostering long-term customer relationships and loyalty.

Best Buy's Black Friday Deals campaign demonstrates how strategic targeting, compelling offers, and integrated marketing efforts across digital channels can drive significant sales and engagement during one of the busiest shopping events of the year.

6.3 Three examples of successful ecommerce campaigns

- *ASOS - Personalized Recommendations Campaign*

ASOS, a global fashion retailer, launched a personalized recommendations campaign on Facebook to drive sales and increase customer engagement. The campaign utilized Facebook's dynamic ads feature to retarget users with personalized product recommendations based on your browsing and purchase history on the ASOS website. By showcasing relevant products tailored to each user's preferences and style, ASOS was able to drive higher click-through rates and conversions, resulting in increased sales and customer satisfaction.

ASOS, a global fashion retailer, executed a highly successful Personalized Recommendations Campaign on Facebook to drive sales and enhance customer engagement. Here's how they implemented this campaign:

- Dynamic Ads: ASOS leveraged Facebook's dynamic ads feature to deliver personalized product recommendations to users based on your browsing and purchase history on the ASOS website. These dynamic ads automatically populated with relevant products tailored to each user's preferences and style.

- Tailored Messaging: ASOS crafted tailored ad copy and messaging to accompany the personalized product recommendations. The messaging highlighted the uniqueness of each product, emphasized its appeal to the individual user's taste, and encouraged them to explore further.

- Engaging Visuals: ASOS utilized high-quality images and compelling visuals in your Facebook ads to showcase the recommended products in an engaging and visually appealing manner. The images were carefully curated to resonate with the target audience and capture your attention while scrolling through your Facebook feed.

- Strategic Targeting: ASOS employed strategic targeting to reach users who had previously interacted with your website or shown interest in similar products. By retargeting these users with personalized recommendations, ASOS maximized the relevance and effectiveness of your ads, increasing the likelihood of conversion.

- Call-to-Action (CTA): ASOS included clear and compelling calls-to-action (CTAs) in your ads to prompt users to take action, such as "Shop Now" or "Discover More". These CTAs encouraged users to click on the ad and explore the recommended products further, ultimately driving traffic to the ASOS website and increasing sales.

- Measurement and Optimization: ASOS closely monitored the performance of your Facebook ads using analytics tools provided by Facebook Ads Manager. They analyzed key metrics such as click-through rate (CTR), conversion rate, and return on ad spend (ROAS) to evaluate the effectiveness of your campaign and make data-driven optimizations as needed.

ASOS's Personalized Recommendations Campaign on Facebook demonstrated the power of tailored messaging, engaging visuals, and strategic targeting in driving sales and enhancing the customer shopping experience. By delivering personalized product recommendations to users based on your preferences, ASOS was able to increase customer engagement, drive traffic to your website, and ultimately boost sales revenue.

Warby Parker - Try-On Experience Campaign

Warby Parker, an online eyewear retailer, launched a try-on experience campaign on Facebook to promote its home try-on program. The campaign featured engaging video ads showcasing the ease and convenience of trying on glasses at home using Warby Parker's virtual try-on tool. By highlighting the benefits of the try-on experience and offering a risk-free way for customers to find your perfect pair of glasses, Warby Parker was able to attract new customers and drive conversions.

Warby Parker, an innovative eyewear retailer, launched a highly successful "Try-On Experience" campaign on Facebook to promote its home try-on program and drive online sales. Here's how they executed the campaign:

- Compelling Video Ads: Warby Parker created engaging video ads that showcased the convenience and ease of your home try-on experience. The videos featured happy customers trying on glasses at home using Warby Parker's virtual try-on tool, highlighting the benefits of the program.

- ➢ Highlighting Benefits: The campaign emphasized the key benefits of the home try-on program, such as the ability to try multiple frames at home for free, hassle-free returns, and access to personalized style recommendations from Warby Parker's team of experts.

- ➢ Educational Content: Warby Parker provided educational content to inform users about the home try-on process and how it works. This included step-by-step guides, FAQs, and customer testimonials to address common questions and concerns and build trust with potential customers.

- ➢ Targeted Advertising: Warby Parker used targeted advertising to reach users who were interested in eyewear, fashion, and online shopping. They leveraged Facebook's targeting options to reach specific demographics, interests, and behaviors, ensuring that your ads were shown to users most likely to be interested in your products.

- ➢ Promotional Offers: To incentivize users to try the home try-on program, Warby Parker offered special promotions and discounts through your Facebook ads. These promotions included exclusive offers such as free shipping, discounts on prescription lenses, or bonus gifts with purchase, encouraging users to take advantage of the offer and try out the program.

- ➢ Engagement and Interaction: Warby Parker encouraged user engagement and interaction with your ads by prompting users to click through to your website to start your home try-on experience. They also encouraged users to share your try-on experiences on social media using specific hashtags, further amplifying the reach of the campaign and generating user-generated content.

- ➢ Measurement and Optimization: Warby Parker closely monitored the performance of your Facebook ads using analytics tools to track key metrics such as click-through rate (CTR), conversion rate, and return on ad spend (ROAS). They used this data to optimize your ads and make adjustments to your targeting, messaging, and creative elements to improve campaign performance over time.

Warby Parker's "Try-On Experience" campaign effectively showcased the benefits of your home try-on program, drove engagement with your target audience, and ultimately drove online sales and conversions. By leveraging targeted advertising, compelling content, and promotional offers, Warby Parker successfully engaged users and encouraged them to try out your innovative eyewear solution.

- *Casper - Holiday Gift Guide Campaign*

Casper, a direct-to-consumer mattress and sleep products company, launched a holiday gift guide campaign on Facebook to promote its products as perfect gifts for the holiday season. The campaign featured eye-catching carousel ads showcasing a curated selection of Casper's products, including mattresses, pillows, and bedding accessories. By targeting users interested in holiday shopping and gift-giving, Casper was able to drive traffic to its website and increase sales during the peak holiday shopping period.

These examples demonstrate how ecommerce brands can leverage Facebook Ads to drive sales, increase customer engagement, and promote your products effectively to a targeted audience. By utilizing personalized recommendations, engaging experiences, and timely promotions, these brands were able to achieve your marketing objectives and drive tangible results for your ecommerce businesses.

Casper, a prominent direct-to-consumer mattress and sleep products company, orchestrated a highly effective "Holiday Gift Guide" campaign on Facebook. Here's how they executed the campaign:

> - Curated Product Selection: Casper created a comprehensive holiday gift guide featuring a curated selection of your mattresses, pillows, bedding accessories, and sleep-related products. The guide catered to different gifting occasions, such as "Gifts for Better Sleep" or "Gifts for Cozy Nights In," offering something for everyone on the holiday shopping list.

- Eye-Catching Carousel Ads: Casper used visually appealing carousel ads on Facebook to showcase your holiday gift guide products. Each carousel card featured a different product with high-quality images, concise descriptions, and clear pricing information, allowing users to easily browse through the offerings and discover gift ideas.

- Personalized Recommendations: Casper personalized the gift guide recommendations based on user preferences, browsing history, and past interactions with the brand. By leveraging Facebook's targeting capabilities, Casper ensured that the ads were shown to users most likely to be interested in your products, increasing the relevance and effectiveness of the campaign.

- Emphasis on Gifting Experience: The campaign emphasized the gifting experience and the joy of giving the gift of better sleep. Casper positioned your products as thoughtful and practical gift options that would bring comfort, relaxation, and better sleep quality to recipients, making them ideal holiday gifts for loved ones.

- Promotional Offers and Discounts: Casper offered special promotions and discounts on select holiday gift guide products to incentivize users to make a purchase. These promotions were highlighted in the Facebook ads, encouraging users to take advantage of the limited-time offers and complete your holiday shopping with Casper.

- Clear Call-to-Action (CTA): Each ad in the campaign included a clear and compelling call-to-action (CTA) prompting users to "Shop Now" or "Discover More." This encouraged users to click through to Casper's website to explore the holiday gift guide further, learn more about the products, and make a purchase.

- Measurement and Optimization: Casper monitored the performance of your Facebook ads closely using analytics tools to track key metrics such as click-through rate (CTR), conversion rate, and return on ad spend (ROAS). They used this data to optimize your ads in real-time, making adjustments to targeting, messaging, and creative elements to maximize campaign effectiveness.

Casper's "Holiday Gift Guide" campaign effectively engaged users, provided valuable gift ideas, and drove sales during the holiday season. By leveraging targeted advertising, curated product selections, and promotional offers, Casper successfully capitalized on the holiday shopping frenzy and positioned your products as must-have gifts for better sleep and relaxation.

6.4 Creative ideas and innovative strategies from real-world practice

Here are some creative ideas and innovative strategies from real-world practice that brands have implemented successfully:

User-Generated Content (UGC) Campaigns: Encourage customers to create and share content featuring your products or brand on social media platforms like Instagram or TikTok. Repurpose this user-generated content in your advertising campaigns to showcase authentic testimonials and experiences, building trust and credibility with potential customers.

- Interactive Ad Formats: Experiment with interactive ad formats such as polls, quizzes, or augmented reality (AR) experiences to engage users and drive interaction with your ads. Interactive elements can increase ad engagement and provide valuable insights into customer preferences and interests.

- Social Commerce Integration: Integrate social commerce features directly into your social media platforms to streamline the shopping experience for users. Enable "Shop Now" buttons, in-app checkout options, or shoppable posts to allow users to discover and purchase products seamlessly without leaving the platform.

- Micro-Influencer Collaborations: Partner with micro-influencers who have smaller, but highly engaged, social media followings within your target niche. Micro-influencers often have a more authentic and personal connection with your audience, making your recommendations more impactful and driving higher conversion rates.

- Live Streaming Events: Host live streaming events or product demonstrations on platforms like Facebook Live, Instagram Live, or Twitch to showcase new products, answer customer questions in real-time, and create a sense of urgency around limited-time offers or promotions.

- Personalized Marketing Automation: Implement personalized marketing automation tools and strategies to deliver tailored content and offers to individual customers based on your behavior, preferences, and purchase history. Use data-driven insights to create hyper-targeted campaigns that resonate with specific audience segments.

- Cause-Related Marketing Campaigns: Align your brand with social or environmental causes that resonate with your target audience's values and beliefs. Launch cause-related marketing campaigns to raise awareness, drive engagement, and demonstrate your brand's commitment to making a positive impact on the world.

- Gamification and Rewards Programs: Incorporate gamification elements and rewards programs into your marketing campaigns to incentivize user participation and foster loyalty. Offer points, badges, or exclusive discounts for completing certain actions such as making a purchase, referring friends, or engaging with your brand on social media.

- Experiential Marketing Activations: Create immersive and memorable brand experiences through experiential marketing activations such as pop-up shops, interactive installations, or branded events. These real-world experiences can generate buzz, drive word-of-mouth marketing, and deepen emotional connections with consumers.

- Content Hubs and Communities: Build online content hubs or communities where customers can engage with your brand, share experiences, and connect with like-minded individuals. Foster a sense of belonging and community among your audience, positioning your brand as a trusted resource and thought leader in your industry.

- AI-Powered Personalization: Utilize artificial intelligence (AI) and machine learning algorithms to deliver hyper-personalized content, product recommendations, and shopping experiences tailored to each individual customer's preferences, behavior, and browsing history.

- Voice Search Optimization: Optimize your website and content for voice search queries to capture traffic from voice-enabled devices like smart speakers and virtual assistants. Create conversational content and optimize for long-tail keywords to improve visibility in voice search results.

- Subscription Box Services: Launch subscription box services offering curated assortments of your products delivered to customers' doorsteps on a recurring basis. Encourage sign-ups through targeted advertising, referral programs, and incentives for subscribers.

- Limited-Edition Collaborations: Partner with other brands or influencers on limited-edition collaborations to create buzz and exclusivity around your products. Leverage the partner's audience and brand affinity to reach new customers and drive sales.

- Storytelling Campaigns: Develop storytelling campaigns that resonate emotionally with your audience, highlighting the brand's values, mission, and impact. Use narrative-driven content across various channels to connect with customers on a deeper level and build brand loyalty.

- Instant Gratification Offers: Offer exclusive instant gratification offers such as flash sales, daily deals, or time-limited discounts to create a sense of urgency and drive immediate action from customers. Promote these offers through targeted advertising and email marketing campaigns.

- Social Proof and Reviews: Showcase social proof and customer reviews prominently on your website and in your advertising campaigns to build trust and credibility with potential customers. Encourage satisfied customers to leave reviews and share your experiences to attract new buyers.

- Virtual Try-On Experiences: Implement virtual try-on experiences or augmented reality (AR) tools that allow customers to visualize products in your own environment before making a purchase. Use Facebook or Instagram AR ads to promote these interactive experiences and drive engagement.

- Localized Marketing Campaigns: Create localized marketing campaigns tailored to specific geographic regions or cultural preferences. Customize your messaging, imagery, and offers to resonate with local audiences and address your unique needs and preferences.

➤ Retargeting and Abandoned Cart Recovery: Implement retargeting strategies and abandoned cart recovery campaigns to re-engage users who have shown interest in your products but have not completed a purchase. Use personalized messaging and incentives to encourage them to return and complete your purchase.

By incorporating these creative ideas and innovative strategies into your marketing efforts, you can attract and retain customers, drive sales, and differentiate your brand in a crowded marketplace.

Chapter 7: Legal and Ethical Considerations

7.1 Adhering to Facebook Ads policies and regulations

Read and Understand Facebook's Advertising Policies: It's essential to thoroughly review Facebook's Advertising Policies and Community Standards to understand the platform's rules and regulations. These policies cover various aspects of advertising, including prohibited content, ad formats, targeting options, and the overall user experience. By familiarizing yourself with these policies, you can ensure that your ads comply with Facebook's guidelines and avoid potential ad disapproval or account suspension.

- Stay Updated on Policy Changes: Facebook frequently updates its advertising policies to adapt to evolving industry trends, user behavior, and regulatory requirements. It's crucial to stay informed about these changes by regularly checking Facebook's official resources, such as the Facebook Business Help Center and the Ads Policies page. Additionally, subscribing to email updates or joining Facebook's advertiser support groups can help you stay abreast of policy revisions and updates.

- Use Authorized Ad Accounts and Pages: Facebook requires you to use authorized ad accounts and pages to run ads on the platform. These accounts must comply with Facebook's terms of service and undergo verification processes to ensure authenticity and legitimacy. Before launching ad campaigns, verify that your ad account and associated pages meet Facebook's requirements to avoid ad disapproval or account suspension due to unauthorized use.

- Avoid Prohibited Content: Facebook prohibits certain types of content in ads to maintain a safe and positive user experience. This includes content that promotes illegal products or services, deceptive practices, discriminatory behavior, or violates intellectual property rights. Before creating ads, review Facebook's prohibited content guidelines to ensure that your ad content aligns with the platform's policies and guidelines.

- Respect Community Standards: Facebook's Community Standards outline the acceptable types of content and behavior on the platform. you must adhere to these standards when creating and running ads to ensure compliance with Facebook's policies. Avoid posting content that violates Facebook's Community Standards, such as hate speech, violence, nudity, or harassment, as this can result in ad disapproval or account suspension.

- Honor User Privacy: Privacy is a top priority for Facebook, and you must respect user privacy and data protection laws when collecting and using personal information for ad targeting purposes. you must obtain explicit consent from users before collecting or using your data for advertising purposes and comply with Facebook's data use policies. By prioritizing user privacy, you can build trust and credibility with your audience while maintaining compliance with Facebook's policies.

- Provide Accurate and Honest Information: Transparency and honesty are essential when creating ad content on Facebook. you must ensure that your ads provide accurate and truthful information about your products or services and avoid making exaggerated or misleading claims. Clearly communicate any terms, conditions, or limitations associated with your offers to set clear expectations for users. By providing accurate and honest information, you can build trust and credibility with your audience and maintain compliance with Facebook's policies.

- Comply with Targeting Restrictions: Facebook has strict guidelines regarding ad targeting to prevent discriminatory practices and ensure a fair and inclusive advertising environment. you must comply with these targeting restrictions and avoid targeting users based on sensitive attributes such as race, ethnicity, religion, or sexual orientation. By using Facebook's targeting options responsibly, you can reach relevant audiences without engaging in discriminatory practices and maintain compliance with Facebook's policies.

- Monitor Ad Performance and Feedback: Continuous monitoring of ad performance and user feedback is essential for ensuring compliance and effectiveness. you should regularly review key metrics such as click-through rates, conversion rates, and engagement levels to assess ad performance and identify any compliance issues. Additionally, pay attention to user feedback and complaints related to your ads and take prompt action to address any concerns. By monitoring ad performance and feedback, you can make data-driven decisions and ensure that your ads comply with Facebook's policies while achieving your advertising objectives.

- ➢ Seek Guidance and Support: If you're unsure about Facebook's advertising policies or need clarification on specific issues, don't hesitate to seek guidance and support from Facebook's support resources or legal professionals specializing in digital advertising compliance. Facebook offers various resources, including the Facebook Business Help Center, support articles, and community forums, where you can find answers to your questions and receive assistance with policy-related issues. Additionally, consulting with legal professionals can provide valuable insights and guidance on navigating complex policy issues and ensuring compliance with Facebook's advertising policies.

By following these detailed guidelines and best practices, you can ensure that your Facebook Ads campaigns are compliant with Facebook's policies and regulations, minimize the risk of ad disapproval or account suspension, and maintain a positive user experience for your audience.

7.2. Protecting user privacy and data

Protecting user privacy and data on Facebook is critical to maintaining trust with your audience and complying with legal regulations. Here are specific steps to ensure the protection of user privacy and data on the platform:

1. **Adhere to Facebook's Policies:** Familiarize yourself with Facebook's Data Policy, Advertising Policies, and Community Standards. Ensure that your advertising practices comply with these policies to avoid account suspension or termination.

2. **Use Custom Audiences Responsibly:** When creating custom audiences for ad targeting, ensure that you have obtained consent or have a legitimate interest in using the data. Avoid using sensitive categories such as race, ethnicity, religion, sexual orientation, or health information for targeting.

3. **Respect User Preferences:** Honor user preferences regarding data collection and advertising personalization. Allow users to opt out of targeted advertising if they choose to do so and respect their decisions.

4. **Provide Transparency:** Clearly disclose how user data will be used for advertising purposes in your privacy policy and ad disclosures. Be transparent about the types of data collected, how it will be processed, and who will have access to it.

5. **Implement Facebook Pixel Safely:** If you use the Facebook Pixel to track user interactions on your website, ensure that you comply with Facebook's Pixel Use Policy. Provide clear information about the use of the Pixel in your privacy policy and obtain user consent where required.

6. **Secure Your Ad Account:** Use strong, unique passwords for your Facebook ad account and enable two-factor authentication for added security. Regularly review and update your account settings to ensure they meet current security standards.

7. **Monitor Third-Party Apps:** If you grant third-party apps access to your Facebook ad account, carefully review their permissions and ensure they have appropriate data protection measures in place.

8. **Limit Data Sharing:** Minimize the sharing of user data with third parties unless necessary for advertising purposes. Avoid sharing sensitive user information and only provide access to trusted partners with clear data protection agreements in place.

9. **Respond to User Inquiries:** Promptly address user inquiries and requests related to privacy and data protection. Provide mechanisms for users to access, modify, or delete their personal data as required by law.

10. **Stay Informed:** Stay up to date with changes in Facebook's policies, regulations, and best practices related to data privacy and advertising. Regularly review Facebook's resources and announcements to ensure compliance with current standards.

By following these guidelines, you can protect user privacy and data on Facebook while still effectively reaching your target audience with advertising campaigns. Prioritizing privacy and transparency can help build trust and enhance the effectiveness of your marketing efforts on the platform.

7.3 Ethics in advertising and avoiding manipulative or harmful practices

Ethics in advertising is a fundamental principle that shapes the relationship between businesses and consumers. This paper examines the importance of ethical advertising practices and provides strategies for you to uphold transparency, integrity, and accountability in your marketing efforts.

- *Understanding Ethical Advertising*

Ethical advertising is the practice of promoting products, services, or ideas in a manner that upholds moral principles and values while respecting the rights and well-being of consumers. It involves adhering to a set of standards and guidelines that prioritize honesty, transparency, fairness, and social responsibility in all aspects of the advertising process. Below are key components of understanding ethical advertising:

- Honesty and Truthfulness: Ethical advertising requires you to be truthful and accurate in your communication with consumers. This means avoiding false or misleading claims about products or services and presenting information in a clear, straightforward manner.

- Transparency and Disclosure: Transparency is crucial in ethical advertising, and you should disclose relevant information to consumers, such as the nature of the product or service being advertised, any affiliations or sponsorships, and the use of persuasive techniques or incentives.

- Respect for Consumer Autonomy: Ethical you respect the autonomy of consumers to make informed choices without coercion or manipulation. They avoid employing deceptive or manipulative tactics that exploit vulnerabilities or undermine consumers' ability to make rational decisions.

- Social Responsibility: Ethical advertising extends beyond individual transactions to consider the broader societal impact of advertising practices. you have a responsibility to promote positive social values, diversity, inclusivity, and environmental sustainability in your messaging and portrayals.

- Compliance with Regulations and Standards: Adhering to legal requirements, industry standards, and advertising codes of conduct is essential for ethical advertising. This includes complying with laws related to consumer protection, truth in advertising, data privacy, and fair competition.

- Consideration of Vulnerable Audiences: Ethical you take into account the vulnerability of certain audiences, such as children, elderly individuals, or individuals with limited cognitive abilities, and avoid targeting them with potentially harmful or inappropriate content.

- Continuous Improvement and Accountability: Ethical advertising is an ongoing process that requires continuous improvement and accountability. you should regularly review and evaluate your advertising practices, seek feedback from consumers and stakeholders, and take corrective action when necessary to address ethical concerns.

Recognizing Manipulative and Harmful Practices

In the realm of advertising, recognizing manipulative and harmful practices is essential for maintaining ethical standards and safeguarding consumer well-being. By understanding these practices, you can avoid engaging in deceptive or exploitative tactics that undermine trust and integrity in the advertising industry. Below are key aspects of recognizing manipulative and harmful practices:

- False or Exaggerated Claims: One of the most common manipulative practices in advertising involves making false or exaggerated claims about products or services. This includes overstating the benefits or efficacy of a product, misrepresenting its features or capabilities, or fabricating testimonials or endorsements.

- Emotional Manipulation: you often use emotional manipulation to influence consumer behavior by evoking strong emotions such as fear, guilt, or anxiety. This can be achievedthrough emotionally charged imagery, dramatic storytelling, or fear-based messaging designed to exploit consumers' vulnerabilities and elicit an immediate response.

- Hidden Persuasion Tactics: Some you employ hidden persuasion tactics to subtly influence consumer decision-making without your awareness. This can include using subliminal messages, product placements, or psychological triggers to manipulate perceptions, preferences, and purchasing behavior.

- Fearmongering: Fear-based advertising relies on instilling fear or anxiety in consumers to persuade them to take a specific action, such as purchasing a product or supporting a particular cause. This can involve exaggerating potential risks or consequences associated with not using the advertised product or adopting a particular behavior.

- Coercive or Deceptive Techniques: you may resort to coercive or deceptive techniques to pressure consumers into making a purchase or taking a desired action. This can include using misleading pricing tactics, creating artificial scarcity, or employing high-pressure sales tactics that exploit consumers' vulnerabilities or insecurities.

- Exploitation of Vulnerable Audiences: Certain advertising practices may exploit vulnerable audiences, such as children, elderly individuals, or individuals with limited cognitive abilities. This can involve targeting vulnerable groups with inappropriate or harmful content, using deceptive marketing tactics, or manipulating your emotions to elicit a response.

- Perpetuation of Stereotypes and Discrimination: Advertisements that perpetuate stereotypes or discrimination based on factors such as race, gender, ethnicity, sexual orientation, or disability can be harmful and unethical. These ads reinforce harmful biases, contribute to social inequality, and undermine efforts to promote diversity and inclusivity.

- Promotion of Unhealthy Behaviors: Advertisements that promote unhealthy behaviors, such as excessive consumption of alcohol, tobacco, junk food, or addictive substances, can have detrimental effects on public health and well-being. These ads may glamorize risky or harmful behaviors and contribute to the normalization of unhealthy lifestyles.

- Recognizing manipulative and harmful practices in advertising requires vigilance, critical thinking, and a commitment to ethical principles. By identifying and avoiding these practices, you can uphold integrity, transparency, and respect for consumer autonomy in your advertising efforts, fostering trust and credibility with your audience while promoting ethical standards in the industry.

Principles of Ethical Advertising

Ethical advertising is guided by a set of principles that prioritize honesty, transparency, fairness, and social responsibility in all aspects of the advertising process. These principles serve as a framework for you to uphold ethical standards and build trust with consumers. Below are key principles of ethical advertising:

- Truthfulness and Accuracy: Ethical you are committed to providing truthful and accurate information in your advertising content. They avoid making false or misleading claims about products or services and ensure that all statements, testimonials, and endorsements are supported by evidence and verifiable facts.

- Transparency and Disclosure: Transparency is essential in ethical advertising, and you should disclose relevant information to consumers in a clear, upfront manner. This includes disclosing advertising intent, sponsorship relationships, and any material connections between you and endorsers. you should also disclose information about product features, pricing, and terms and conditions to help consumers make informed decisions.

- Respect for Consumer Autonomy: Ethical you respect the autonomy of consumers to make informed choices without coercion or manipulation. They avoid using deceptive or manipulative tactics that exploit vulnerabilities or undermine consumers' ability to make rational decisions. you should empower consumers with accurate information and give them the freedom to choose products or services that align with your needs and preferences.

- Social Responsibility: Ethical advertising extends beyond individual transactions to consider the broader societal impact of advertising practices. you have a responsibility to promote positive social values, diversity, inclusivity, and environmental sustainability in your messaging and portrayals. They should avoid promoting harmful or offensive content and strive to contribute to the well-being of individuals, communities, and society as a whole.

- Compliance with Regulations and Standards: Adhering to legal requirements, industry standards, and advertising codes of conduct is essential for ethical advertising. This includes complying with laws related to consumer protection, truth in advertising, data privacy, and fair competition. you should stay informed about regulatory changes and ensure that your advertising practices are in compliance with applicable laws and guidelines.

- Respect for Cultural Sensitivities: Ethical you recognize and respect cultural differences and sensitivities when creating advertising content. They avoid using stereotypes, derogatory language, or culturally insensitive imagery that may offend or alienate certain audiences. you should strive to create inclusive and culturally relevant ads that resonate with diverse audiences and reflect the values and aspirations of different communities.

- Accountability and Integrity: Ethical you take responsibility for the ethical implications of your advertising decisions and actions. They operate with integrity, honesty, and accountability, and are willing to address any ethical concerns or complaints raised by consumers or stakeholders. you should uphold high ethical standards in your advertising practices and maintain the trust and confidence of your audience.

By adhering to these principles, you can demonstrate your commitment to ethical advertising practices, build trust and credibility with consumers, and contribute to a more transparent, responsible, and sustainable advertising ecosystem.

Strategies for Ethical Advertising

Ethical advertising requires a proactive approach that prioritizes honesty, transparency, and consumer welfare. you can implement various strategies to ensure your advertising practices align with ethical principles and standards. Below are key strategies for ethical advertising:

Consumer Education

Empower consumers with critical thinking skills and media literacy education to help them recognize and resist manipulative advertising tactics.
Provide educational resources, such as fact-checking guides, critical consumption tips, and online courses, to help consumers make informed decisions and navigate advertising messages responsibly.

Industry Collaboration

Collaborate with industry stakeholders, regulatory bodies, and consumer advocacy groups to establish and enforce ethical advertising standards and guidelines.
Participate in industry forums, workshops, and working groups to share best practices, address emerging ethical issues, and promote transparency and accountability in advertising.

Ethical Decision-Making Frameworks

Implement ethical decision-making frameworks within organizations to evaluate advertising practices, identify ethical dilemmas, and make responsible choices that prioritize consumer well-being.

Develop internal policies, guidelines, and protocols that outline ethical principles, standards, and procedures for creating, reviewing, and approving advertising content.

Monitoring and Enforcement

Establish mechanisms for monitoring advertising practices, investigating complaints, and enforcing consequences for violations of ethical standards.

Implement regular audits, reviews, and assessments of advertising campaigns to ensure compliance with ethical principles, industry standards, and regulatory requirements.

Transparency and Disclosure

Be transparent about advertising intent, sponsorship relationships, and any material connections between you and endorsers.

Clearly disclose relevant information to consumers, such as product features, pricing, terms and conditions, and any potential risks or limitations associated with the advertised products or services.

Engagement and Dialogue

Foster open and honest communication with consumers through engagement channels such as social media, customer feedback mechanisms, and consumer helplines.

Listen to consumer feedback, address concerns or complaints promptly, and take corrective action to rectify any ethical issues or lapses in advertising practices.

Ethical Advertising Campaigns

Develop advertising campaigns that promote positive social values, diversity, inclusivity, and environmental sustainability.

Align advertising messaging with ethical principles and societal needs, and avoid promoting harmful or offensive content that may undermine consumer trust or well-being.

- *Employee Training and Education*

Provide training and education to employees on ethical advertising principles, practices, and compliance requirements.

Empower employees to raise ethical concerns, seek guidance, and escalate issues to management or compliance teams when necessary to ensure ethical advertising standards are upheld.

By implementing these strategies, you can demonstrate your commitment to ethical advertising practices, build trust and credibility with consumers, and contribute to a more transparent, responsible, and sustainable advertising ecosystem.

Conclusions

Using Facebook ads can be a highly effective strategy for businesses to reach their target audience, drive engagement, and achieve their marketing objectives. Here are some key conclusions about using Facebook ads:

1. **Wide Reach:** Facebook boasts billions of active users worldwide, providing advertisers with a vast audience to target across various demographics, interests, and behaviors.
2. **Targeted Advertising:** Facebook's advanced targeting options allow advertisers to reach specific audiences based on demographics, interests, behaviors, and even interactions with their brand.
3. **Cost-Effective:** Facebook ads can be a cost-effective advertising solution, particularly for small and medium-sized businesses with limited budgets. Advertisers can set their own budgets and bid strategies to control costs and maximize ROI.
4. **Diverse Ad Formats:** Facebook offers a variety of ad formats, including image ads, video ads, carousel ads, and more, allowing advertisers to choose the format that best suits their marketing goals and creative assets.
5. **Engagement and Interaction:** Facebook ads provide opportunities for engagement and interaction with users through likes, comments, shares, and direct messages, fostering brand awareness and customer relationships.
6. **Measurable Results:** Facebook's ad platform provides robust analytics and reporting tools that allow advertisers to track the performance of their campaigns in real-time. Advertisers can monitor key metrics such as reach, impressions, clicks, conversions, and return on ad spend (ROAS) to measure the effectiveness of their ads.
7. **Customization and Optimization:** Advertisers can customize their ad campaigns based on their objectives, target audience, creative assets, and budget. They can also optimize their campaigns through A/B testing, audience segmentation, and ad creative refinement to improve performance over time.
8. **Integration with Other Platforms:** Facebook's advertising ecosystem integrates with other platforms such as Instagram and Audience Network, allowing advertisers to extend their reach and engagement across multiple channels.
9. **Challenges and Considerations:** Despite its benefits, using Facebook ads comes with challenges such as ad fatigue, ad relevance, ad blindness, and changes in

platform algorithms. Advertisers must stay informed about industry trends, best practices, and platform updates to adapt their strategies accordingly.

In conclusion, Facebook ads offer businesses a powerful platform to reach and engage their target audience, drive brand awareness, and achieve marketing objectives. By leveraging advanced targeting options, diverse ad formats, and robust analytics, advertisers can optimize their campaigns for success and maximize their return on investment. However, it's essential to stay vigilant, adaptable, and ethical in your advertising practices to ensure long-term success on the platform.

www.ingramcontent.com/pod-product-compliance
Lightning Source LLC
Chambersburg PA
CBHW062108220526
45471CB00010B/3646